88x50

A MEMOIR OF SEXUAL DISCOVERY, MODERN MUSIC AND THE UNITED STATES OF AMERICA

ADAM TENDLER

This is a memoir based on true events. I consulted journals, interviews, emails, press clippings, pictures, videos and audio recordings to recreate its scenes and dialogue as faithfully as possible. To protect privacy, I have changed some names and re-arranged some settings.

ISBN: 0615700098

ISBN 13: 9780615700090

Library of Congress Control Number: 2012949535
Dissonant States Press, Barre, VT

for Shadroui
"fuck the notes"

MISS ME

    I dislike it when someone famous dies, and all of the representatives sit there and make speeches saying, "I'm sure that _____ would want us to go on and not be sad." That's not true. Anyone who dies would definitely want people to be sad, and rock things up... at least I will. I'll tell my representatives (since I'll be a star) to tell everyone to NOT get over it, and be sad, all except for my family. If no one misses me, I'll be alone and forgotten within a week. That's not what I want, baby. I want everyone to miss me, miss me, miss me, miss me!!!

Growing up in Vermont, I wrote stuff like this all the time. I imagined my eyes as a camera through which the world would someday see the movie of my life. I would escape, and I would live in that movie. Piano lessons were just a thing I did. I didn't practice, and for years begged my mom to let me quit, only sticking with it because she bribed me with trips to Burger King after my lessons. I owe my life in classical music to a double cheeseburger.

    I was still playing out of kiddie books when it came to my attention that I was not just a dabbling musician and the star of my own movie, but also something people called a "faggot." I didn't know what it meant, that word—only that it was bad. Any word chanted behind me in the hallway had to be bad. Any word framed within an accusation had to be bad. Any word whispered between the seats of the bus, woven sensually into the fabric of a threat, had to be bad. But as for the specifics, I was stumped. Sex—and what's sex again?—with other boys? "But how?" I remember asking my mom and two older sisters. "How does that *work?*"

I was eight.

By my early teens, I got the picture, and though I lived in fear—fear of violence, fear of hearing that word, fear that they were right, that something *was* different about me—I compensated for the fear by constructing an elaborate fantasy world, maybe another movie, in which everything I did carried some kind of profound weight, had its own long line of intention that would lead, someway, somehow, to some kind of ultimate success in the future. Retribution. It didn't matter how; I just needed to ensure that someday I'd be special in a *good* way, for a *good* reason, not just for being that word.

Raised on the sunnier side of classical music, I never felt an urge to play standard repertoire, and picking up on this, my piano teacher started exposing me to the less famous works of Chopin, and then Rachmaninoff. Something clicked. The music, so emotional—I insisted on minor keys—resonated with me, and the fact that the notes were right there on the page made it somehow accessible. All I had to do, essentially, was access it. I delved into this music with a voracity that surprised everyone—my teacher, my family, even myself—and from the Romantics I moved into the Modernists, from

Prokofiev to Schoenberg, then to Copland. It excited me that *those* notes, those dissonant notes, were on the page. That someone chose them, wrote them down, and that somehow I totally understood them. As the dissonance stacked, it seemed increasingly clear that I was starting to express myself at the keyboard, which worked out perfectly well because I suddenly had a creative outlet that didn't involve opening my mouth and suffering the same old consequences, hearing about my girly voice, hearing that word.

It was a game of necessity and escalation, my beginnings as a musician, of escalating responsibility to meet each increasingly demanding piece with the preparation required. I started to do what my piano teacher had begged me to do for nearly a decade: practice. By the time I hit high school, I practiced twelve hours a day—scales before school, repertoire throughout the day whenever I could escape class, and run-throughs of my conservatory audition program all night, staying late in the chorus room of my high school as janitors locked the building around me.

I became a phantom to my classmates and family, but earned a spot at Indiana University School of Music, one of the country's best, and yet still, when I got there, something was missing. I didn't feel any momentum, no direction. Even as I played my way to the top of the class, I still felt like the same child playing from kiddie books and bargaining lessons for cheeseburgers. I wanted to prove myself still, to disappear completely into music only to someday explode out and into the world in a way that people would remember, a blizzard of notes falling around me like confetti, re-birthed, transformed—an artist—special in a good way. I also understood that this kind of apotheosis required something big, something new, something cinematic. "But how?" I wondered. "How does that work?"

I graduated from IU a semester early, with honors, and with no prospects whatsoever. Living briefly in New York City in the apartment of a recently deceased great aunt—all of her dresses were still festering in the closet—everything I tried to do flopped, from day jobs to night jobs, auditions, internships, getting management, and so on. I returned home to Vermont defeated, with one last-ditch idea: a tour. Yes, a big tour. Fifty states. I'd always wanted to travel, I loved modern American music, and I had nothing else to do. I would call it America 88x50—eighty-eight keys by fifty states.

It was early 2004, and I created a small proposal, or what I thought was a proposal, and sent this lofty credo to arts councils in all fifty states. It went something like this:

I intend to perform a solo piano recital comprised entirely of modern American music in each of the fifty United States. The project relies on the adjustment of conventional ideas concerning the formal recital and recital hall, as I will offer the performances for free to any venue that accommodates. I have set my audience requirement to a minimum of one person.

The recital program represents the diverse perspectives of four American art-music pioneers—Charles Ives, Charles Tomlinson Griffes, Alberto Ginastera, and Aaron Copland—composers whose distinct lives and pursuits forged the paths for virtually all American composers who followed, whose work often unconsciously anticipates later musical trends that span genres and generations. Such expressions range from the abstract, the popular, the minimalist, the cynical, the impressionistic, the exotic, to the influences of jazz and Pan-American folklore.

I aim to share, discuss, and experience the music of this recital program—staggeringly unique and largely ignored by the mainstream classical establishment—with individuals who, for any number of reasons, will particularly value the opportunity to witness it live, up close, and in their communities, from a performer invested in their response. Ultimately, I wish to cultivate an honest dialogue between artist and audience rooted within the American music presented in this program.

American artists must consider the widely neglected but mutually important roles of individuals both allied with traditional art culture and those who—by any circumstance—stand disconnected from it. This negligence has alienated both communities and left each deprived and respectively misunderstood. Thus, any concentration toward actively clarifying the perspectives and responsibilities of both the country's artistic circles and its general public will help to resolve the dilemma that presently divides the two, encouraging mutual perception, association, and definition to each community's roles and accountabilities.

On a personal level, the project symbolizes a comment on and a protest against the norm imposed upon most

*twenty-first century artists; the expectation that commands
individuals within the arts to either compromise their integrity by submitting to the industry of illusory competitions, or
indefinitely trap themselves within the walls of academia,
or to superficially commit their time and spirit to general
workplaces far removed from their training and expertise...*

I'll admit it was a pretty good speech, a half-bitter,
half-inspired, half-baked product of my post-conserva-
tory circumstance, full of bombast and holes. And, perhaps worse, it was merely a front, a grandiose web of
half-truths hiding a murky, undulating, formless morass
of unspoken, maybe unspeakable, rationales pulsing
and thumping like an overheating engine locked in a
closet, launching me ecstatically out onto the highways
of America with barely a vision of how, what, why, where,
and who would say, "Yes."

Fifty manifestos hit fifty desks in fifty states, and then
nothing happened.

I started e-mailing and calling presenters that I'd
find on haphazard Google searches. I'd look at a map of
any given state, see an area or town that intrigued me,
maybe a nice name, maybe a pretty-looking park, and
then I'd go from there. Any and every lead I received
helped to shape the route I might take for the tour—
might, because for the most part, presenters thought I
was crazy, or worse, an amateur. I hadn't the heart to tell
them I felt like both.

Speaking of plans, my health insurance plan, an
extension of an extension courtesy of my mother's work,
was set to expire in just over a year, and as a sufferer of
ulcerative colitis, a disease that first struck at IU during

a particularly stressful string of performances, I needed insurance. It seemed I only had a brief window during which I could safely perform America 88x50 before—and I hated to admit it—I'd have to find a job that gave me insurance, an expressly non-bohemian fate within which I was sure I'd never have the freedom to try anything like this again.

I applied for grants and was universally rejected. It seems they wanted me to have a plan, too. I didn't have the time to wait for another granting cycle, or the time to really create that plan, so I decided to fund the tour myself, substituting at local public schools, teaching piano lessons, and working construction with my step-father at a landfill on the Canadian border, bringing my scores to the jobsite, memorizing passages visually, and practicing them at night when I got home—piecing together my whole program this way. If I had access to the Internet during the day, say, when substituting at a school, I'd e-mail more proposals to more potential concert hosts. "Clearly, you are not a professional musician," one presenter wrote back.

But ideally someone would say yes, and ideally I would lodge with my hosts while on the road, and if not with them, in motels, hostels, campgrounds, or with friends and family. I also hoped to sustain the project financially by selling homemade CDs at my shows, a compilation of live performances from my IU days. I had a headshot taken at the same studio that did my high school senior pictures, and I traded my Chevy truck, bought during college with inheritance money from my late grandfather, for a little blue Hyundai Tiburon. My stepfather and I gutted the keyboard out of my grandfather's upright piano and built a wooden box around it so I could practice (silently—it had only the action, no strings) on the road. This apparatus had a handle for carrying and a lid that unhinged to expose the keys. It looked like a coffin.

By May 2005 I had a little less than $8,000 in the bank and a small handful of concerts, maybe five, disparately located and inconveniently timed—New Mexico one day, followed by Maryland a few days later, then a few empty weeks until the next show—but I needed every "Yes" I could get. I'd leave for my first concert in early June and arrange the rest of the tour from the road, and then just see how far I could get. That, honestly, was the closest thing I had to a plan.

HOW TO READ THIS BOOK

I've supplemented the text with pictures, sound, video, and expanded passages, accessible via hyperlink for some e-reading devices and signaled by footnotes for print editions. You can access all footnotes at www. dissonantstates.com/88x50footnotes. Feel free to access these materials at any point and in any order; however, I encourage exploring them either at chapter breaks or after reading the whole book so as to avoid interrupting the reading process.

America 88x50[1]
Adam Tendler, piano

Three-Page Sonata[2] (1905)....................Charles E. Ives
    Moderato   (1874–1954)
    Andante–Adagio
    Allegro, March Time (but not a March – Rollo)

Three Tone-Pictures[3], Op.5 (1910–12).........Charles Griffes
    The Lake at Evening   (1884–1920)
    The Vale of Dreams
    The Night Winds

Sonata[4] (1917–18, rev. 1919)

Doce Preludios Americanos[5] (1944)..........Alberto Ginastera
    Para los acentos   (1916–1983)
    Triste
    Danza criolla
    Vidala
    En el 1er modo pentafono menor
    Homenaje a Roberto Garcia Morillo
    Para los octavas
    Homenaje a Juan Jose Castro
    Homenaje a Aaron Copland
    Pastoral
    Homenaje a Heitor Villa-Lobos
    En el 1er pentafono mayor

(short pause)

Four Piano Blues[6] (1926–48)....................Aaron Copland
    Freely Poetic   (1900–1990)
    Soft and Languid
    Muted and Sensuous
    With bounce

Piano Sonata[7] (1939–41)
    Molto moderato
    Vivace
    Andante sostenuto

---

1 http://media.dissonantstates.com/a/88x50-Soundtrack
2 http://media.dissonantstates.com/a/IvesThreePageSonata.mp3
3 http://media.dissonantstates.com/a/GriffesThreeTonePictures.mp3
4 http://media.dissonantstates.com/a/GriffesSonata.mp3
5 http://media.dissonantstates.com/a/GinasteraDocePreludiosAmericanos.mp3
6 http://media.dissonantstates.com/a/CoplandFourPianoBlues.mp3
7 http://media.dissonantstates.com/a/CoplandPianoSonata.mp3

PART ONE

POUGHKEEPSIE, NEW YORK

Dotti was dead by the driver's side door.

Fresh yellow shit seeped from her backside and had smeared across the cement of the garage floor, matted into her tail. Her mouth was shaped into a sneering grimace, teeth shockingly exposed. I dropped my suitcase and crept toward the little white dog's body, positioned as if it was guarding the entrance to my little blue Hyundai, and with my eyes fixed on her, almost as if she might run away, I collected a garbage bag from my stepfather's nearby workbench and slowly bent over her, grabbing her by the collar. I'd been making continuous trips to the car from the house all morning, and just minutes before this grisly discovery, Dotti had been poised upright, watching me attentively as I packed the car. In an instant she'd become alien and unrecognizable, curled up and misshapen into some kind of rude object.

Still functioning automatically, in a state of shock and a little bit annoyed because this was moments before I was supposed to leave for Poughkeepsie, four hours away and the first show of my alleged fifty-state tour, I lifted Dotti's already stiff corpse by the collar and began gagging as it swung before me. After seventeen years, it felt too soon to be holding her in the air this way. An irrational impulse inside me assumed she was choking, and that I was killing her. I fumbled the garbage bag open, let her go, and with a thud Dotti disappeared and collided against the concrete floor. I spun the bag closed and placed it in a corner. I would bury her after I finished loading the car.

Walking out of the tomb of the garage and across the porch toward the open front door, I heard something now pounding over and over inside the house, a faint, almost pitched, hollow tapping, and when I looked inside, I saw a blackbird fluttering and smashing itself headfirst against a window, trying to escape. It must have flown into the house the moment I began attending to my dead dog. I grabbed a broom and chased the bird around the house until it finally flew out the front door again. It was a bright blue Vermont morning, and the blackbird sat perched on a tree limb, watching me as I balanced the broom and caught my breath in the open doorway. I had to finish packing. I had to get to Poughkeepsie. I had to bury my dog. I had to forget that my tour began this way.

Was it six hours later? Approaching the entrance to a large darkened theater, I heard Jo Ann's voice from behind me. "No." I stopped. "In here! In here," she called. I turned around, but she'd already disappeared into a side parlor, a kind of sitting room with a baby grand piano in the front[1], its chipped legs indenting the kind of gray carpeting you might find in an airport terminal. I walked up to the instrument and began touching around. It looked nice, but the soft pedal made a loud clapping sound every time I pressed it, and the F above middle C kept ringing even when my finger came off the key.

"How is everything?" she asked. "Will it be okay for your concert?"

"It's great!" I chirped back, and she left me to practice.

An hour later a man and a woman walked in. "Why's it set up like this?" he asked, looking at the rows of chairs.

"I don't know," she answered, as if thinking about something else. Neither of them seemed to notice me. "Actually, I *do* know," she corrected herself. "There's a guy doing a piano recital in all fifty states and the first show of the tour is here!"

I sat at attention.

"Oh," he muttered, and they both walked out.

I'm in a bathroom stall. I pull a tight black shirt over my chest and fasten a hand-me-down Coach belt around my black pants. In a few minutes, Jo Ann will introduce me to an audience of about fifteen people. I don't know a single one of them. They came to see me

1 http://media.dissonantstates.com/i/CunneenPiano.jpg

play a piano recital. They believe me. They think I'm real. A real pianist.

I shine my black boots with two sweaty palms.

In minutes, I'm lurching over the keyboard, working with all my energy to play the correct notes. Sweat rolls down my temples and drips onto the piano keys. I can't see my audience, but I imagine them wincing. Who am I but some odd pianist laboring before them, hammering through an already-dissonant program, rising from the bench, swinging and swaying, engaging the rhythms from my inside out? But between the pieces, they clap. After I introduce each work, they clap. When I finish the program, they clap, and they stand. They still believe me. They want to know more about the music, the project, and about me. Do I have a website? A blog? An agent? A recording of me playing this program? No, no, no, and no.

Many people ask when I first started playing. I can't remember, but say what I always say. "I don't know. Maybe six or seven?" I'm too shy to direct anyone to the stack of CDs I'm selling, which I placed on a chair in the corner.

MORGANTOWN, WEST VIRGINIA

I never really liked West Virginia. Every time I'd ever passed through the state, people (at gas stations, mostly) treated me like I was some kind of outsider, clearly a Yankee, clearly an intruder, clearly a *something else*. But Morgantown looked promising, a college town with an overflowing topography of steep streets, green plateaus, a mantle of small mountains and sudden cliffs that just barely accommodated its residents. My venue, the Monongalia Arts Center, looked like it could have been

Town Hall, and in front of the granite steps leading up to it stood a kiosk with a huge poster inside. My headshot was blown up to almost life-size proportion, and below it was a detailed description of my tour, mostly lifted from the e-mail proposal I'd sent a few weeks earlier. I stood before the kiosk frozen in place. This is really happening, I thought.

When I walked inside, a woman greeted me from a front desk. "Can I help you?"

"I have a recital here tonight," I said.

"You're one of the performers?" she asked.

"It's just me, a solo recital. My picture's outside."

It was a small black box theatre. The piano[2], a Steinway, was placed before five or six rows of unfolded metal chairs with cushioned seats. A ruddy wooden floor creaked below my sneakers. I put my hands on the edges of the black fabric covering the Steinway and lifted it like a skirt, then opened the lid and started practicing, uncomfortably, as a janitor watched. My chest became tight. I couldn't breathe. My elbows felt glued to my sides, and when I came to a fast passage, my whole arm tensed and sent my defenseless fingers splaying across the keyboard like a figure skater crashing into the ice. I would hold my breath even more, my heart burning, stomach aching. Crumbling inside. Confidence gone. I'd forgotten how to play. I wished the janitor would go away.

---

2 http://media.dissonantstates.com/i/MonongaliaPiano.jpg

Standing before the crowd, I thought only one thing: Fuck. There were children everywhere, their parents sitting beside them, everyone glowing with expectancy. I had visions of them rising to their feet midway through the concert, grabbing the kids, and stomping out of the hall, betrayed by America 88x50, by some nobody kid performing a program of music they'd never heard of and would probably never choose to hear again. And here they'd hoped to inspire their kids with some Chopin or Mozart or Beethoven, and I was playing Ives[3]. But I had to remind myself that these folks came to the recital knowing full well what I'd play; they'd read the newspaper article[4], they knew the deal. And if not, weren't these exactly the people I was hoping to share this music with, people who had never heard it before, children included? I had a full house.

The concert ends with a collective sigh. Someone says "Wow," and then there's the first clap. Then more. Then they don't stop. Some people disperse. Some approach. A man pats me on the back like a coach congratulating his quarterback. "We need a little dissonance sometimes!" he says. "It might sting a little, but it's good for you, like a stiff drink. You have to get used to the taste, but then you learn to appreciate it. You start looking forward to the sting." A little boy jumps in the air and clutches the hand of his bearded father, and

3 http://dissonantstates.com/post/9534542860/
thedayiplayedforcharlesives

4 http://media.dissonantstates.com/i/WestVirginiaArticle.jpg

they squeeze by the greeting line to the restroom just behind me. My presenter crouches to the boy. "Do you want to go home and learn the piano, now that you've heard Mr. Tendler?" His eyes bulge with fright and he shakes his head no.

When I drive away, a truck squeals by my Hyundai and the voice of an old man shrieks from inside, "Go back to fuckin' Vermont." West Virginia says goodbye.

☆

The next day, I stop at a buffet restaurant some-where between Cleveland and Columbus for lunch. Sitting alone, I feel a quiet, restrained energy in the air, and while chewing, I study the families, hunting parties, and young couples who have gathered here. A group of men wearing camouflage caps and dark shirts with airbrushed wilderness scenes on them erupt into laughter, shattering the silence of the restaurant, and my heart jumps; I nearly drop my fork. They're laugh-ing at me. They have to be laughing at me. I throw some cash on the table and walk fast, very fast, out the door, noticing a dirty diaper stuffed into a cigarette depository.

In the Hyundai, I sail past kids playing on neon-colored plastic swing sets, wives in sundresses bringing lemonade out to their dirt-caked husbands, and faded billboards that announce each exit's fast-food chains, jutting into the air from a farmland that's otherwise calm and flat and emerald green. They have an organic quality, these signs, weathered enough to appear as if the fields actually grew them.

Behind me I have my eyes set on a Chevy Blazer with oversized tires and New Hampshire plates. The driver makes the same moves as me, swerves with me, passes cars with me. It's like we have a secret pact, a kinship, and he trails me so closely that I can see his rearview mirror ornaments. I'm protecting him. If we encounter a cop, I'll get pulled over first.

It's okay. We remain a pair, racing past slower drivers and somber gas stations[5]. I want to know his story, his hometown, where he's going, everything about him. Will he follow me off the interstate if I exit? I need gas, after all, and there's a station coming up. I hold my breath, signal right, slow slightly, and watch my rearview for his corresponding blinker. In a brute motion, he dodges the back of my Hyundai and careens onward. Rejected.

BLOOMINGTON, INDIANA

I was rejected by every school I auditioned for except IU, which is something I always lied about to my friends there. I *did* audition for Juilliard, as well as New England Conservatory, Cleveland Institute of Music, Peabody Conservatory, Eastman, Curtis, and even Harid Conservatory in Florida. Unanimously, unequivocally, universally rejected.

I even considered my acceptance to Indiana a kind of fluke. The admissions office lost my application and preliminary audition tape, which I was only reminded of after all of my other rejections had arrived in their

---

5 http://media.dissonantstates.com/i/GasStation.jpg

tidy white envelopes. A kind of last-ditch effort, I contacted IU to see what had happened to the materials I'd sent, and they apologized—"We don't know how this could have happened!"—and invited me out for a private, late audition for the piano department chair. My mom and I drove to Bloomington from Vermont and I played terribly, probably my worst audition yet. So when the chair of the piano department leaned back in his chair and said I was accepted into the music school, using the word "potential," I figured he meant "guilt"—guilt that I'd traveled so far because of an error on the school's behalf.

This haunted me throughout my years at IU, and as much as I practiced, performed, and made a reputation for myself as a diligent student, an intellect, and a firm player, I always figured I'd merely hustled myself into one of the best music schools in the world, slipping successfully through the cracks. Every day I fought to make sure no one would find out my secret, but this frenzied state of overachievement only escalated my paranoia, reaching a fever pitch at my senior recital hearing (in a hearing, the faculty requests excerpts of a program, grades the performance and then gives the green light for the recital) where I made tons of mistakes onstage, forgot the notes to important passages, and failed. No green light. After ripping down all the posters for my recital that I'd already posted across the school, I took to my dorm room and had the closest thing to a nervous breakdown that I'd ever experienced, almost dropping out a week before graduating. It was like I still didn't know how to play. My teacher told me that my brain hadn't caught up to my body. I'd put in the work, earned my technique, but my *mind* still didn't believe I could do it.

I needed to create my own classroom. But first I needed to get out. I replayed my senior recital hearing, passed, performed the recital, completed my exams—at that point I was taking mostly graduate-level classes—and left Bloomington with honors a semester early, skipping the winter graduation ceremony. They could mail me my degree.

It was like I'd never left. All my trapped memories[6] of IU were awakened again, released like a blood blister, from the time the piano faculty converged to discuss expelling me for posting obscene recital advertisements (featuring images from Madonna's *SEX* book), to the time I stood trial for rigging copy machines to spit out free copies for my homework assignments. I drove from street to street in what felt like a recurring dream. In every sense, I'd been here before. I knew what would happen next. If I got out of my car at such-and-such spot I would smell such-and-such smell, or if I walked into such-and-such building I'd see such-and-such person.

I wandered through the dim, asylum-like hallways[7] of the music practice building, the "Annex," as it was called, hearing that unmistakable mélange of muffled sound you only hear at a conservatory, fading in and out like a strange dream—operatic sopranos shrieking up

6 http://dissonantstates.com/post/9879824844/indianafragment
7 http://media.dissonantstates.com/i/Asylum.jpg

the scale and colliding with other sopranos, trumpets, pianos, cellos, a pile up of sounds. I walked through this cave of horrors like someone who'd just returned to a bicycle for the first time in years, nervous but discovering within seconds that nothing had been forgotten, that I still guarded myself with that ghostly silence I'd maintained during my school days, going through the motions of shielding my tiny practice room window with a folded piece of paper so that no one could look in and see me playing.

But I hadn't come back for a stroll down memory lane. No, I came back to IU because I needed an Indiana concert for the tour and, quite frankly, this would do. I had an old friend reserve Recital Hall[8] for a "recording session," and I scrawled the concert info onto some pieces of paper and taped them up all over the school.

Dimming the lights myself, I took the deepest breath I could, one that would fill my rumbling abdomen, my wet armpits, and my tight neck, and I exhaled this tension as best I could. I approached the one-hundred-dred-year-old Steinway[9] in the center of a stage which creaked beneath my feet. The instrument's great jaws opened wide to reveal golden strings that poured light into the room like a treasure chest. There were four people in attendance, all of them friends, sitting at the extreme corners of the hall. As I sat, the air conditioner switched on automatically—it had always been so

---

8 http://media.dissonantstates.com/i/RecitalHall.jpg

9 http://media.dissonantstates.com/i/IUPiano.jpg

loud—drowning out a security alarm beeping outside in the lobby—were we breaking and entering?—and the pipes groaning within these ancient walls. I shattered the ambience with my trembling left hand, playing the opening interval of the *Three-Page Sonata* like a death knell, an immovable drone that sounded mostly like an accusation. Remember me?

CHICAGO, ILLINOIS

"You gay pussy dumb-ass motherfucker!"

My cousin lambasts a friend and I'm startled to attention, my boggled eyes catching a helicopter as it zooms by the living room window with a spotlight on Lake Michigan. It disappears into the jungle of skyscrapers with their sparkling exteriors. Chicago at night. I stand up slowly and stride through the party with the awkward self-consciousness of a drunk, leaving a trail of footprints behind me in the soft white carpet. Once out of view, I reach out to both sides of the hallway and guide myself along to the bathroom, as if supporting the walls from falling in on me. After peeing, I clutch at the fuzzy air around the toilet until finding the nozzle to flush. I'm fucked up. Now back in the living room. "Missouri scared me," says a girl next to me. "They like, had no teeth."

"Is that so?" I slur. Had we been talking? "It looks like we're going out." I point to a crowd congregating by the door.

In the elevator, a guy asks where I performed that afternoon. "People's...? People's Music School. They offer, like, free music lessons to...um..."

And now we're in a cab. The world goes by like a slide show, a succession of still images. If I turn to look at something, the image seems to trail behind the movement of my skull, like my eyes need time to catch up. The city is in fast-forward, and my head helplessly bobs and flops around in the backseat, passing cars and streetlights looking less like objects and more like laser beams in a hyperkinetic lightshow. Now we're in a club. "He's on tour doing piano recitals..." my cousin explains. "...*Piano recitals!*" he screams, since his friend can't hear over the music. "But not like, classical music. Modern stuff. Wild stuff, like..." He pantomimes a crazy person playing the piano.

I try to think back to earlier that day, how we'd walked to the People's Music School on a cracked, dirty sidewalk, stepping over men with their backs leaning against rusty garage doors pulled over the empty shops. How my cousin and I stopped to watch a guy breakdancing to the static fuzz of a boom box. How the school was brand new, how I tilted my head upward to look at the sunny balconies encircling the atrium where my performance would take place, floor after floor of walkways lined with doors of frosted glass—practice rooms, someone explained, each with a piano—and how onstage there were two young students shining the Mason and Hamlin baby grand piano I would play. How I waited offstage as the director introduced the concert, providing an almost apologetic assurance to those thirty people who had come. "He has only attracted a small group of you here, but I assure you he is of the highest quality." How I chewed my lip because this "small group" had been one of my biggest audiences yet. And how, during the Charles Griffes *Sonata*, an old woman in the front row, sitting serenely in her wheelchair, shit her pants.

HOPE, ARKANSAS

I was almost at the Missouri state line when lights flashed behind me in red, white, and blue. I pulled over and waited for the officer, a bronzed woman with black hair and a badge almost as shiny as her French manicure, to walk leisurely to my window.

"Do you know why I stopped you?"

"I may have been speeding?"

"I clocked you at seventy-nine in a sixty-five."

"Ah."

"Where are you headed?"

"Hope, Arkansas."

She started to giggle. She must have seen the Vermont plates. "What are you doing all the way down there?"

"I'm playing piano recitals in all fifty states," I replied, waiting for her reaction. "American music," I added. She nodded. "So, my next recital is in Arkansas."

"I'm giving you a citation," she said.

The ticket shook me into setting my cruise control to the speed limit, and for the rest of the trip the landscape passed by like a diorama, as if on a conveyor belt, and I sat in the driver's seat, idle, like a passenger to my own driving. It was evening when I finally began to see Arkansas license plates, brute and plain with the state name stamped on a white background in thick, masculine red letters. Curtains of pine trees lined both sides of the interstate, only rarely opening to reveal a Super Walmart or a row of dilapidated houses, or a brand new church that looked like a castle.

☆

Mike and I had our choice of several open parking spaces in the desolation of downtown Hope. When we stepped out of his BMW convertible, our voices seemed to bounce against the brick buildings. He was my concert host for the night—literally, my recital would take place in his living room, organized by a local arts council—and he was taking me out to lunch at Cherry's, a kind of soda fountain that represented one of the few surviving businesses I could see. We walked in and each customer stopped to watch our slow procession to an empty booth. Settling in—or was I squirming?—I picked up a menu, noticing several pictures on the wall of Bill Clinton. "Does Clinton ever come back here to his hometown?" I asked.

Mike seemed to struggle with an answer. "In short, no." I waited. "I mean, he's come back a couple times. Myself, I'm a Republican who doesn't much care for Clinton."

I started looking at the menu. "I'm thinking grilled cheese."

"We're more proud of the *reputation* that a president grew up in Hope," continued Mike, "than of the person himself."

"Okay."

"This'll interest you!" he said, sitting up. "I taught music appreciation this summer and today was the final class."

I took my eyes from the menu. "What did you listen to?"

"Oh, some Debussy, Stravinsky. A little Copland."

"Which Copland?"

"*Appalachian Spring, Rodeo, Fanfare for the Common Man...*"

"Yes, well, those are important pieces," I said.

"Very diplomatic of you," Mike laughed. "Well, all of my students, without me saying a word about Copland or the pieces, *knew* it was American music!"

"The Copland I'll play tonight might be a little less obvious," I said. "But I guess that's sort of the point."

"That's all right." He sighed, "You know, I wonder who decides which modern pieces 'stick,' so to speak, and which ones sink away into obscurity?"

I didn't answer because I didn't know. "The answer might be in your curriculum!" I joked.

When we returned outside, I looked around, shading my eyes. "So this is Main Street?"

"This is the Old Main Street," Mike confirmed.

"Is there a *new* Main Street?"

Mike laughed. "This is downtown, but most of the business moved out toward the highway. You probably saw it. All those big stores?" He stopped, and then continued with a little trepidation, as if confiding a secret. "Say what you will, but one of the *good* things about all those box stores out there is that no one can really compete with them. No one's really that wealthy around here. Local businesses can have monopolies, too, you know." He looked around at the empty square. "But it does leave the old downtown looking like this, which is a shame. What's one to do?"

I didn't answer because, again, I didn't know.

I put the piano bench to its maximum height but, still too low for me, retrieved a hardcover anthology of *Southern Living* from the kitchen to use as a booster. Mike's living room had a shiny black Kawai grand. Everyone who had shown up so far looked similar to him, which is to say, Republican, and to my surprise, hardly anyone knew about my tour, namely, my goal to hit all fifty states. They just came to the concert because someone from a local arts council had invited them, a woman named Repha[10] who, up until today, had been my only point person in Hope. I didn't know about Mike until that morning, let alone that my concert would take place in his living room.

An older man greeted me with a grin and vigorous handshake. "So I understand you're gonna play some pretty music for us. It's not gonna be *too* contemporary, is it?"

"No, no," I answered confidently. "All the composers are dead."

A small crowd sat on chairs and sofas encircling the piano, and the Kawai and I burned together in the middle like a campfire. When the pedal came up after the final, quiet notes of the program, the Copland *Sonata*, I saw a woman facing me from across the room sink into her chair with a relieved, sensual smile. This was modern music.

After the show, people approached me with compliments and questions, and nearly everyone bought a CD, my first sales so far. Mike also handed me a check for a staggering $200. "To benefit the Adam Tendler speeding ticket fund," he announced. Some people asked me to sign their discs. I did so reluctantly. In my mind, I was still a know-nothing pianist masquerading as a kind of

10 http://dissonantstates.com/post/10392413533/balladofrepha

musical Johnny Appleseed, performing obscure modern American music for people who knew very little about it and who might not know the difference between a triumph and a train wreck. This tour was a debut of convenience, it seemed, an ego-driven attention magnet at best, and at worst—and so far—a publicity stunt without the publicity. Couldn't anyone see that? Didn't anyone want to know why—really why—I was out here alone on the highways of America?

KANSAS CITY, MISSOURI

A murmuring came from the stall next to mine. Every time someone flushed, a message, barely-audible, floated through the smoky air of the truck stop restroom, and I sat in my stall, staring through the grayish yellow air at crushed cigarette butts and black ash soaking in urine on the floor, straining to hear his whispers through the muffled classic rock coming from dusty amplifiers in the ceiling. Someone flushed again. Yes, he was speaking to me, inviting me over. My stomach curled up and seemed to press against my spine. Now, in each hanging silence, *I* was the one flushing, impulsively testing my neighbor to see if I could get another message, then another, like I was feeding quarters into a jukebox. The thrill fell somewhere between titillation and revulsion, a feeling I knew well.

Transfixed, my mind flashing through all of the possible outcomes of going over there, I finally resolved to flush a final time and scurried from the stall. That blend of fear and arousal still tickling in my lower back nearly sent me running out the bathroom door, as if a ghost was behind me, chasing me into the soda aisle. And that's where I lingered, at least for a little while, because part of me wanted to see him. Not so much to determine whether or not I should have taken him up on his offer, but because I just wanted to see his face. Just to see.

To pass the time, I made small talk with an employee, asking if she knew of any pianos in this town called Peculiar. She shook her head. "Can't think of any pianos in Peculiar. Maybe a church?" My eyes kept darting to the bathroom door to see if he, or anyone else, was coming out. But no one ever did. Not while I was there.

In a cheap motel on the outskirts of Kansas City, I'm looking at pictures on my laptop. Straight porn, as it were, anything to erase the restroom episode from earlier today, and I'm working away at myself like a teenager. But I don't finish. I won't. I rarely do. I haven't finished in months, paranoid that an orgasm might poison my music, make my delivery of it somehow less urgent. I tell myself that I play best when I want to fuck everyone in the audience, the composers themselves, the notes on the page. I tell myself that I like to play when I'm backed up and ready to burst. So I edge for hours, teetering on the point of release, and then stop, saving myself for America 88x50.

I pulled in front of an Oriental rug store with a Steinway in the window and pulled a promotional photo and CD from the trunk. When I opened the huge glass front doors, a Shih Tzu trotted toward me, and then a dark older man helping two elderly customers in the back looked my way. He appeared about forty years old, longish slicked black hair with gray streaks, purple tank top, and a gap in his teeth. He left the couple to their decision and approached me, extending a hand, his voice soft and smooth. "Name's Bruce[11]. Can I help you?" I told him about the tour.

"Ah," he smiled and tilted his head back like I'd reminded him of something familiar. Then he stopped, eyebrows furrowed. "So wait, what is it you're doing?"

I explained the tour again.

He scratched his chin. Then Bruce had an idea. "We have a First Friday every month on this street. The galleries stay open late, thousands of people walk around, and most places feature music or something." He motioned toward the grand piano[12] in the window. "I usually sing and people just come in and out, but you could do something instead, I imagine."

I agreed, and then stopped myself short. "But does that mean…"

"Yeah, that means you're playing tonight."

I spent the afternoon practicing in a nearby park on my silent keyboard. Curious spectators stopped to watch and I'd take the opportunity to invite them to the concert. When I returned to the store, I saw that Bruce

11 http://dissonantstates.com/post/9922583332/balladofbruce
12 http://media.dissonantstates.com/i/KansasCityPiano.jpg

had set up a small display at the entrance, a side table with concert programs, a stack of my CDs, and a jar to put donations in. My glossy, black-and-white headshot rested against a vase stemming with white flowers. I told him I liked it, but that it also looked like I'd died and this was my memorial[13].

"The arts are in real trouble," he said a few minutes later after brewing us some tea. "I mean, we have an okay art scene here. A lot of galleries and so on. But there's no classical music. It's so exclusive that no one hears it." I told him about the generally positive responses I'd gotten from audiences so far, and how this had actually surprised me.

"People are just hungry," he said. "I sang twelve Schubert songs one Friday and the people, they just came in and were, like, awed. Farm boys, art folk...it didn't matter. They just ate it up. It was like, as if suddenly *Schubert* was radical music. We all went through this transcendental experience with it. And that's what's important, I think, in music. When it stops being music and it turns into something more. More than music."

Bruce crossed one leg over the other, shaking it like he had some kind of nervous twitch. The heel of his cowboy boot tapped on the floor. I asked why he bought the Steinway. "I went to school, but," he shook his head, "I just went crazy. It was like, little boy coming to the city. I smoked a lot of pot and didn't take advantage of the opportunities I could've had. The singing thing," he motioned to the piano, "I've only come back to it in the past eight years, since my partner died." There was silence. "Of AIDS," he continued, answering a question

---

13 http://media.dissonantstates.com/i/Memorial.jpg

I didn't ask. "So I put the piano in here so that every First Friday I'd *have* to sing." He brought his gaze back to me. "I sort of do what you do. We have to make it for ourselves, right? Even though people...*artsy* people, they come in here and they think, 'Well, he deals rugs, he must do well, so what right does he have to get involved with *our* scene?' That kind of thing rubs off on me. I have an upcoming performance with the Civic Opera singing Mahler." He shrugged. "Inside, I still feel like an imposter."

"I understand," I said.

He squinted his eyes with a dubious expression, like he knew something better than me. "Maybe you're just scared to acknowledge your gift, like I was. Because if you accept it, then you have a responsibility not to waste it."

The little whispers, the footsteps, the people entering and leaving and staring through the window, unhinges my mind away from its usual mid-performance task of turning the next note into some oppressive mystery— *are you sure?* And with my mind distracted and the addiction to self-test and self-destruct out of the way, my playing happens almost automatically, even beautifully. I'm not thinking anymore.

A man enters wearing a polo shirt, khaki shorts, and sunglasses. His wife, whom I only see in the corner of my eye, is dressed in something bright green. "Oh, my *God!*" she shrieks, probably surprised, maybe even charmed, by the scene she's stumbled upon—a piano recital in an Oriental rug store. "Bill, look at these *rugs!* My *God!*" By now, Bill has begun circling behind me, looking at rugs but mostly chatting on his cell phone, which has already rung twice during the softest of my Ginastera preludes[14].

"Yeah, so where are you? Oh, we're in a rug store. Oriental rugs. Yeah, a flying carpet store! We're getting a flying carpet! Going *awaaaaaaaaay* on a flying carpet!"

A male voice from the audience shudders, "Please!"

SPENCER, IOWA

On Fourth of July weekend in Iowa, the houses I passed were bedazzled with miniature flags and tiny red, white, and blue lights. I stopped at a Walmart in the north-eastern lakes region and bought a small children's tent for seventeen dollars. There were no overtly childlike designs on it and the dimensions seemed safe. Basically I needed to save cash. With a confirmed concert in South Dakota the next week and nowhere to play till then, I headed toward this area because it was, for one, on the way, but also because it looked pretty on my atlas, with tree symbols everywhere—campgrounds where I could stay for cheap while waiting or, at best, hustling an Iowa show into the works. The last town before the touristy Lake Okoboji[15] area was Spencer, and I kept my eyes peeled for possibilities. I saw an art gallery called Arts on Grand and, just across from it, a piano shop. Reason enough to park the car.

---

14 http://media.dissonantstates.com/a/GinasteraPentafonoMenor.mp3
15 http://dissonantstates.com/post/927550761/iowa#okoboji

The locked piano store had no customers or staff inside, only a cat lounging behind the window, which drew my attention to a poster taped from the inside advertising something called the Spencer Concert Association. I studied the poster and found a phone number. It was 4:45 on the Saturday afternoon of Fourth of July weekend, but I called anyway. After a few rings, a man's voice answered. "Hello?"

I had to have the wrong number. "Is this...uh, the Spencer Concert Association?"

He introduced himself as Michael, said that I'd called him at home, and then admitted that, yes, he more or less *was* the Concert Association. "You're interested in tickets?" he asked. "We don't have any concerts until the fall."

"No. I want to *play* a concert," I said. "This week."

He invited me to his house down the street. Spencer in general was a little run down, but Michael had a beautiful and massive brick house. He met me outside on his walkway smelling like aftershave. He wore bright plaid shorts and an unbuttoned shirt.

I pitched him America 88x50 in the front yard and, to my astonishment, he was receptive, telling me that he wanted to change Spencer's image from that of Iowa's leading meatpacker to that of an artist colony. "But we need artists to come here," he said. In ten minutes we decided on Thursday for the recital.

That night I dined with Michael and Josh[16], a man whom I presumed to be his lover, at a pizza parlor

---

16 http://dissonantstates.com/post/9795682170/someiowafragments

overlooking the lake traffic, trunks bleeding the desperate, non-descript thuds of muffled bass, rims spinning with shining silver. I was in Iowa? Kids hung out of windows as their sullen parents navigated through the traffic with boats swinging from trailers behind them. Far off, I could see an amusement park with bumper cars, a Tilt-a-Whirl, and a roller coaster.

Josh had bulging muscles and a flattop haircut, like a drill sergeant. He seemed restless as Michael and I made surface small talk, in fact talking very little about the concert. I kept hinting at the small tent I'd just erected down the road at the White Oaks Campground, fishing for an invite to stay in Michael's small mansion, and eventually he offered the bed in his guest room for the day after tomorrow, since the campground made me sign up for two days on account of the holiday weekend.

So Josh and Michael are lovers, I kept thinking. All my scattered experiences, from five years old up, had been covert affairs. I wasn't sure I'd ever really seen a same-sex couple out in the open. They emanated the kind of old familiarity that most people would long for with a loved one, and yet, while it was at once so normal and so right, it also just seemed incredibly odd to me. So when they made love, there was no sinking-ship feeling of regret and defeat afterward? It seemed impossible, so ingrained was repentance in my own routine. I could remember all the way back to the second grade, explaining to my best friend at the time that, if we introduced the physical element into our friendship, we would run the risk of an awkward dynamic afterward. By the time I reached IU, I was completely paranoid and totally celibate, and that's when I started restricting my orgasms, and that's when I was diagnosed with colitis[17].

Closet? What closet? One doesn't name his denial because one never knows his denial—that is, until after the fact. I trusted that my own discomfort with the *idea* of a closet, or with Michael and Josh holding hands in front of me, was some kind of sign that, deep down, I was straight as an arrow. I'd dated girls—yes, with effort, but I'd done it—and whatever *other* experiences I'd racked up and kept secret were just an addiction, and addictions can be broken, beaten, or at least covered up. I could persuade others to believe anything I myself believed in. Isn't that how it worked, and hadn't I done it before? Didn't I get into IU that way? Wasn't I in the midst of a piano recital tour, somehow convincing everyone in sight I was a concert pianist just because I said so and decided to act like one?

My tent was right next to the street[18], the only available spot left at White Oaks Campground, its sign illuminating the inside of my tent like a Chinese lantern. Rocks jabbed into my hips and back, and I bunched up a thermal shirt to cushion my body against the ground. I felt entombed. The tent narrowed at both sides, so any movement I made either pushed my temple against a side wall or snagged my feet and shoulders. If I turned on my side, I was millimeters away from suffocation.

---

17 http://dissonantstates.com/post/10812861315/colitiscuts
18 http://media.dissonantstates.com/i/CarByRoad.jpg

Then I remembered I needed to take my colitis meds. My forehead wedged in the tent ceiling, I foraged in my bag for a silver pen to puncture the foil of my cyclosporine pills, derived from a Norwegian fungus and used for transplant patients (my body was basically rejecting its *own* colon). The pills smelled horrible, and my tent instantly smelled like a skunk. I gathered up the little pink eggs into my palm, along with four Imuran tablets, three Colazols, a Rowasa enema to do in the morning before my shower, and a Canasa suppository for right now. I swallowed the pills, applied the suppository, and lay down. Then there was a clap of thunder, and then a downpour. After just a few breathless minutes of awful anticipation, a drop of water finally landed on my forehead. I sat up and again collided with the ceiling of the tent, smearing my forehead with cold water. There was nothing to do, so I lay back down, held myself with arms crossed in the sleeping bag, and fell asleep.

It was the morning of my recital when I came into Michael's kitchen, from the warm and dry guest bed, to see my face printed on the local newspaper's front page, and then an even bigger portrait on the inside with an accompanying article[19]. "It's so serious," I said to Michael, marveling at the page. He was standing at the kitchen table, perhaps uneased by my lack of enthusiasm, since he himself had been so pleased with the publicity he'd drummed up. Indeed, this Spencer show probably had the most media attention of any America

---

19 http://media.dissonantstates.com/i/ObligationFulfill.jpg

88x50 recital yet. But Arts on Grand only had an old upright piano, and piano recitals, so I thought, just didn't *happen* on upright pianos. I'd tried the instrument the day before—it stood almost as tall me—and I thought it sounded like a honky-tonk player piano in a novelty shop. And yet here I was, this week participating in interviews with radio stations, agreeing to photo shoots, papering the town with posters, and now reading about myself in the paper. "I hope people like it after all this fuss," I finally mustered.

Michael urged me not to worry. "In Spencer, everyone gets a standing ovation."

The upright looked more grotesque now than I'd remembered, hunched like a monster in the middle of the purple gallery[20]. I felt more nervous for this recital than any other so far on the tour, a pit heavy in my stomach, and I knew it had less to do with the music or all my unplanned shows (thirty-something?) and everything to do with this piano.

I noticed somebody had made carrot cakes, and an older woman came forth with pitchers of water and iced tea to place on a picnic table in the back of the gallery. A photographer from the paper appeared and asked me to sit at the piano before people entered so that he could take a picture of me that would appear the next day on the front page of Spencer's Daily Reporter[21]—the second day in a row my face would grace the cover of the local paper.

---

20 http://media.dissonantstates.com/i/ArtsOnGrand.jpg

21 http://media.dissonantstates.com/i/SpencerNewspaperPhoto.jpg

People began to enter, and I said "Hello" and "Thank you" to most of them as they found their way to the foldable wooden seats Michael had set up around the piano before setting up a video camera. Inside I groaned. Video documentation[22]? He came up behind me and whispered that the concert had sold out. Thirty-three people.

In the performance, I worked furiously at the piano, delving my head into the keyboard like a mechanic under the hood. Was it beautiful? I don't know. Did I play all the right notes? Ha![23] But for a recital exclusively devoted to twentieth-century music and an audience comprised almost exclusively of old ladies, it worked.

I got a standing ovation.

I'm in a messy dorm room, but also in my old elementary school in Vermont. The building staff wants me to leave so they can lock up for the evening. I have friends waiting for me outside in a car and we're all going to the airport for a big trip. I make it to the lobby but realize I've left my wallet in the dorm room. I find an older man who looks like a coach and he lets me return upstairs. I can see this special treatment annoys the rest of the staff, and even my friends, whom I glimpse outside. Once back in the room, I can't find my wallet. There's too much pressure. The room spins as I search, and now I begin to remember other things I've forgotten, keys and clothes and books, all scattered and lost in this spinning room. I hear car horns honking from outside. First I hear one

22 http://www.youtube.com/watch?v=FNe0GZR0Rwc

23 http://dissonantstates.com/post/927550761/iowa#mistakes

group of horns, then another, and then a third group, building and mounting until there's a chorus of fat, dissonant chords, ear-shredding, clashing, and overlapping in a slow, rhythmic ebb and flow. After only a couple seconds, I feel it. I'm about to have an orgasm. Intoxicated by my power—this is music for *me*—I feel my loins pulse and throb with the horns, the bubbly tickle of euphoria swelling from my groin down my legs. I don't care about my wallet or the airport or my friends or the coach or the staff because I'm in control and they all want me, need me, and all I want or need is their music, their angry music, to keep feeding me, nourishing me. I grab a chair behind me with both hands, brace my body, lean back, and in that spinning room I come.

I wake up with my shorts heavy and thick. I sigh in relief. I feel like a real musician. Finally, I have something to show for it.

FLANDREAU, SOUTH DAKOTA

It was a three-hour drive across 90 and up 75 to the Royal River Casino Bingo and Motel in Flandreau, South Dakota, a frontier-looking town of roughly two thousand people where, tucked along Second Avenue, was the Crystal Theatre[24], an old movie house with a sky-blue marquee. I stopped the car. On street level, where the movie posters would normally go, I discovered a huge sign[25] with my picture on it and a detailed narrative of the America 88x50 program and its composers.

---

24 http://media.dissonantstates.com/i/CrystalTheatre.jpg

25 http://media.dissonantstates.com/i/CrystalPoster.jpg

Aaron Copland, it explained, was the composer responsible for "the theme for American beef commercials."

I drove onward to the casino, which was enclosed in
nondescript concrete like the outside of a high school
gymnasium. I parked the Hyundai and in a moment was
dropping my things beside the king-size bed and three
chairs of my room. I went in search of the buffet. The hallway carpeting[26], with its river-like design, carried me first
toward the casino, a dark, vast room that shouted with
bells and sirens, flashing lights, and jangling coins. The
hallway walls were decorated with massive murals[27] depicting pow-wows and historical battle scenes, and traditional
banners hung from above. So this was an Indian reservation. I took a right and floated into the buffet, loading my
tray with fried chicken, egg rolls, and lasagna; the Crystal
Theatre set me up with free meals here, and I prepared to
make the most of it. I presented my voucher to the cashier, an older woman with slicked gray hair. She took it and
started searching my face. "You're the pianist?"

"How'd you know?" I shouted, and a table of dreary
diners turned their heads toward us. I covered my
mouth and repeated softly, "How'd you know?"

"The voucher, for one!" she laughed. "And ya
look like you're not from around here." She began
rummaging under her cash register. "Plus, I saw an
advertisement for your show. Bet I got it right here."
She pulled out a small newspaper and started tearing
through the pages. "Yes! Right there!" She folded it
back to show me a black-and-white, text-only ad[28] that

26 http://media.dissonantstates.com/i/HallwayRiver.jpg

27 http://media.dissonantstates.com/i/CasinoMural.jpg

28 http://media.dissonantstates.com/i/WantedAd.jpg

looked sort of like a WANTED poster. "And I read an article[29] about you, too, in another paper, but there were never any pictures." She was still studying my face, smiling. "Guess I just thought you'd be much older! You're...what..."

"Twenty-three."

About a month before, I contacted a man named Terry in Flandreau who almost immediately booked me at the Crystal Theatre, which he ran. His voice over the phone put me at ease, something about the way he answered his phone. "This is Terry!" He was a big man who, when I met him outside the theater a couple hours before my concert, greeted me with a hearty Midwestern handshake, smiling wide under his white moustache and revealing several gold teeth.

It was indeed an old movie theatre, with bright red seats[30], a little balcony, and a small stage in the front, which today had a shiny Boston baby grand in the center. "Rented her today from down in Sioux Falls," said Terry, nodding toward it.

"Do you show movies still?" I asked.

"Not so much anymore. We tried, but just couldn't compete. The movies we got were old and pretty bad." On my way in, I'd noticed a poster for the 1992 Steve Martin and Goldie Hawn comedy, *Housesitter.* "It's too expensive to get the new movies other theaters get. We just can't afford it." He put his hands on his hips and

29 http://media.dissonantstates.com/i/FlandreauArticle.jpg

30 http://media.dissonantstates.com/i/Crystal-Inside.jpg

shook his head, still smiling. "And too bad, too. I mean, look at this." He opened his arms to the stage.

In the third movement of the Ives, when the music turns from a polyrhythmic march into a broken rag-time[31], I listen for the customary giggles. Nothing. Maybe at the end of the piece when, in accordance to Ives's own tongue-in-cheek instructions for the pianist (not found in any printed edition, but only in the manuscript), I cross my arms to play the final C-major chord—maybe then they'll laugh. No. Not today.

Moving on, the Griffes pieces sound great on this new piano, exotic and pristine, soft colors and floating mists, and I deliver the Ginastera *Preludios* in a wild, throbbing, virtuosic, schizophrenic display. Muted applause.

It's intermission, and time for some serious on-the-ground politicking. I walk up the aisle to meet and greet my audience. Immediately, I receive a vigorous handshake from a man who introduces himself as Tony. "Tony Firman! This is wonderful! Just wonderful!" His family glows beside him. "Why don't you stay with us tonight? Or if not, you can have breakfast with us all in the morning and then be on your way to—to wherever you're going next!" He laughs and slaps me on the back. "In Flandreau, you always have a place to stay at the *Firm Inn!*"[32]

---

31 http://media.dissonantstates.com/a/IvesBrokenRag.mp3

32 http://dissonantstates.com/post/1180394198/southdakota#firminn

An elderly woman sitting with her husband motions me to come over. She takes my hand in hers and says, trembling, "You play so beautifully." I thank her.

Two boys approach. "Do you play piano?" I ask. They nod. "Is your teacher here?" They shake their heads. "Do you like your teacher?" They nod. "I loved my first teacher[33]," I say. "Do you practice?"

First nothing, then they squirm. One answers, "Not really in the summer."

"I never liked practicing in the summer either," I say, scrunching my face.

Terry's voice shoots from behind me. "Adam practices in the summer, but he calls it performance!"

America 88x50 was a loss for the Crystal Theatre. The turnout for the concert covered only about a quarter of the cost of renting, delivering, and tuning the piano. Meanwhile, I had forty bucks in my pocket from CD sales. I offered to give it back, but Terry said no, rolling up the gigantic poster for my concert. "We don't get culture, or at least *this* kind of culture," he gently shook the rolled-up poster in his hand, "into a community like Flandreau overnight. You chose us because people don't come here to play these kinds of concerts. The more they do, the more people will come. That's why I said yes to you, and those of us who came tonight won't forget it. You made a big impact." He handed me the poster as the neon-lit beer logos that blocked the windows of Flandreau's tiny bars[34] began lighting up like fireflies.

33 http://dissonantstates.com/post/1180394198/southdakota#shadroui
34 http://media.dissonantstates.com/i/Bars.jpg

INTERNATIONAL PEACE GARDENS, NORTH DAKOTA

A narrow highway glided through fields of goldenrod stretching for miles in every direction, and rays of sunlight broke through the clouds, looking bigger and brighter, as if I was closer to the sun up here in the North Dakota highlands[35]. At the furthest end of the highway straightaway[36], the pavement melted into sky like a shimmering mirage. Then I hit Canada, because even though half of it lies in North Dakota, the entrance to the International Peace Gardens is in Manitoba, about a half-hour drive from the nearest town in the US. I followed a series of handwritten signs past manicured fields, enormous statues[37], ponds, and fountains, until I reached the headquarters of IMC, or International Music Camp[38], a summer program that attracts students from across the world, and that invited me to serve as a guest faculty in conjunction with my America 88x50 concert, which would close piano week. Many of my students would be only a few years younger than I was.

There's Leah, who asks me while puzzling over her music, "So is that like a sharp or a flat or whatever?" And Timothy, who suffers a nervous breakdown when I

---

35 http://media.dissonantstates.com/i/Highlands.jpg

36 http://media.dissonantstates.com/i/Straightaway.jpg

37 http://media.dissonantstates.com/i/PeaceGardens.jpg

38 http://dissonantstates.com/post/10569551595/northdakotafragments

use a pen in his score: "If it's in pen, then during piano exams my teacher will see I couldn't do that part! Pencil erases!" And then Kristopher, stunningly effeminate, who holds his music books (which reek of secondhand cigarette smoke) tight across his thighs when he walks. Nathan contorts his mouth when he plays Liszt. Raef only plays new age music. Alexandra shrugs her shoulders when I ask if she even likes playing the piano. Julia flirts to deflect from the fact that she can't play Beethoven's *Pathetique.*

And then there's Tim, eighteen years old, just out of high school, with a mop of curly blond hair that falls around a chiseled face. He moves with a pack of admirers who loiter outside my studio cabin door while I teach. I don't stop them. In our lessons, I guide Tim through some songs he's written, smoothing out the progressions, giving suggestions on voicing, and on the far wall of my studio he and his friends have drawn a likeness of me on a chalkboard, my shirt reading "I ♥ piano," and an arrow pointing to me like I'm a scientific example: Mr. Tendler[39]. In our most recent session, he mentions a faculty colleague of mine, also named Adam. "So is he gay or what?" he asks, smirking.

It's as if, with this question, asked about someone else, Tim has punched his fist through my chest and plunged it down deep into my intestines. "I mean, with the bleached hair... And, you know, now he says he's going to be a *priest!*" Tim belts a belly laugh that seems to shake the dust out of the cabin's dirty screen windows. "Listen, listen," he continues, crouching forward in his seat as if to confide the most important clue to

---

39 http://media.dissonantstates.com/i/Chalkboard.jpg

his case, the last puzzle piece—but it's nothing; he's just sharing an inside joke. "If me and my friends think someone's gay, we either do a thumbs-up, a thumbs-down, or a thumbs sideways." Tim gestures accordingly. "We give Adam a thumbs-sideways because of the priest thing, just to give him benefit of the doubt."

I feel myself growing hot with rage. *What "thumbs" am I, Tim?* I want to ask. *A thumbs up? A thumbs sideways?* But mixed with the anger is envy, because Tim will never have to know what it feels like for someone like Adam. Someone like me. And I envy that. Tim will never run from a Daytona strip club during his spring break, sobbing because all his friends could talk about their lap dances with glee, discuss the erections they'd maintained, while he only sat helpless and shriveled like a baby as a naked breast brushed his face. Tim will never lie to his family doctor to obtain a Viagra prescription just so he can date girls and avoid explaining to them why his body won't respond. That was last year; I told the doctor my colitis meds had ruined my libido, a side effect I made up, and I told the girls I dated that I couldn't get it up because of all the stress of organizing America 88x50.

I could hear them, an eager audience of several hundred, plus some scattered community members, waiting for the concert to start as I lingered in the wings of the stage. The camp director introduced me to a surge of applause so staggeringly loud it blasted away any anxiety I may have ever had.

Cameras flashed from the darkness as I played, and over the music I could hear gasps and laughter and cheers, like a laugh track in a television sitcom. A standing ovation and the thunder of stomping feet followed each piece.

With the concert over, I retreat offstage and crack a side door for some air. I see several older people walking to their cars. Regular folks. Not IMC people. A red-cherry sunset[40] begins to streak its pink light across the sky. "I'm glad we didn't pay for *that*," one of them says, and I close the door as if it's revealed a terrible secret. My mind scans the entire program, all the mistakes I made, the too-louds and too-softs, the wrong notes... and suddenly the wash of applause, the stomping feet, the screams of my students are all meaningless, a bunch of kids cheering. Biased kids.

I want to get out of here. Out of these clothes. Out of this camp. I begin looking for an escape—*not through that door!*—but I can't go anywhere. The camp director is onstage announcing Dorm of the Week.

BIGFORK, MINNESOTA

I was running on fumes when I pulled the Hyundai into an ancient gas station in the sleepy town of Northome, Minnesota. There were digital lights glowing in orange on each manual pump indicating grade and price, but

---

40 http://media.dissonantstates.com/i/Sunset.jpg

no lights on inside the actual station. I walked up to the front door, and inside was a stocky young man mopping, probably a few years younger than me, wearing a camouflage tank top. I pulled the door open, jangling a set of rusted bells dangling above my head. Their clumsy sound brought the boy's eyes up to meet mine. "Help you?"

"Are you open?" I didn't enter.

"Nope. Just cleaning. That you on pump two?"

"Yes. Is there anywhere I can still get gas?"

"How bad ya need it?"

"I'm completely empty. Heading to Bigfork."

He laughed. "Well, you're screwed then!"

I scratched my head. "What should I do? Really."

"You got a credit card?"

"Yeah."

He sighed, his eyes wandering upward, as if consulting the ceiling. "Okay, hold on." He placed the mop against the wall and went behind the counter, pushed some buttons, and looked up to me. "All right, pump away!"

I thanked him, and just before the door closed between us, I heard his voice.

"So what the hell's in Bigfork?"

I caught it with my foot. "I'm playing a piano recital there."

He looked surprised, but said nothing, then focused again on his mop.

"So how far away is it?" I asked.

"First you hit Effie, and that's probably about thirty miles or so."

"And there's no gas station between here and there?"

"Not a damn thing 'tween here and Effie."

☆

Patricia looked like Jackie Kennedy. I saw her waiting for me at the end of a long driveway, standing in
the doorway of her house, which was shaped into two
domes[41]. I could hear a river[42] babbling somewhere on
the property as I stepped out of the Hyundai. "And you
have a river flowing down through your backyard!" I
cried, coming to her.

"It flows up," she answered, shuttling me inside.
"North to Canada. You arrived just in time for dinner.
Bear—Bear's my husband—and some of his former law
students just came back from a fishing trip, so we're having trout. And please. Call me Patty[43]."

Bear sat at the head of the table wearing a tie-dyed
Rolling Stones shirt, and a braided ponytail fell from
behind his otherwise bald head. I mostly listened as he
and his students bickered playfully, talking law, defend-
ing their arguments, and one-upping each other with
specific cases and obscure laws. My silence may have dis-
appointed Patty, who probably expected some interesting stories from the visiting "troubadour" at the table,
as she called me, but I preferred to listen. In doing so I
learned that Patty had choreographed for the Minnesota
Opera and used to teach piano in the garage apartment
where I'd sleep, all before creating the state-of-the-art
Edge Center in the tiny village of Bigfork, population

41 http://media.dissonantstates.com/i/Domes.jpg

42 http://media.dissonantstates.com/i/BigforkRiver.jpg

43 http://dissonantstates.com/post/10346652376/balladofpatty

hovering just over four hundred. It would be my venue the next day. Bear, I learned, still taught and was working on his ninth book. They took immense pride in their work, and especially in their ability to maintain a cosmopolitan sensibility out here in the sticks. "I'm sure we have the only bidet north of St. Paul," Patty said gladly.

The next day, as I hammered out some technical drills on the upright piano in my garage apartment, there was a loud snap and a B-flat went firing off the keyboard, the slender black note tumbling onto the rug and staring back at me like an amputated finger. In mashing my stiff, under-practiced digits into the keyboard, I'd broken the fucking piano.

I'd have to leave early for my concert to find some Super Glue in town, wherever "town" was, and then I'd reaffix the key later in the cover of night. I would not, and did not, ever say a word to Patty or Bear about what I'd done to their piano.

☆

The Edge Center[44] looked like a gargantuan minimalist art project against a gray sky thick with clouds and twilight—beige in color with three connected cubes, sections that were each taller and bigger than the one before it, like a staircase for Paul Bunyan, whose full-color statue just so happened to be standing right there in downtown Bigfork.

---

44 http://media.dissonantstates.com/i/EdgeCenter.jpg

Patty, who had been at the Edge all day choreograph-
ing for her upcoming production of *The Music Man*,
showed me to a large dressing room with vanity mirrors and a basket full of fruit and granola bars. "That's
all for you!" she said, motioning graciously toward the
basket. I wish I'd known. After my Super Glue run, I'd
consumed a bag of potato chips and an orange soda in
the front seat of my Hyundai, engine off, in the Edge
parking lot. The classical musician prepares.

The grandiose hall had enough bells and whistles
to rival almost any opera house. It was what I saw lurching in center stage that stopped me dead in my tracks:
another upright[45], a real monster, waiting in a cloak of
cobwebs. Patty had warned me, but this was beyond anything I'd ever imagined. I approached the piano with
the forced nonchalance of someone visiting a friend in
the intensive care unit, reaching out to its keyboard as if
taking that friend's hand. The notes either clicked like
castanets, made no sound at all, or were so out of tune
that it was inconceivable how any audience would deci-
pher anything coming out of it. The music of America
88x50 could just as well have been *Fur Elise*. I opened
the top of the piano with a terrible creak and, sitting
down, slid open the wooden window level with my face,
the place where one would usually place their music,
to expose the strings. Maybe it would help the sound. I
took a deep breath, blew into the hammers, and a century's worth of dust exploded back into my face. I got up
and walked away. All this phantasmagoria had me, for
the first time since beginning the tour, seriously considering cancelling a concert.

---

45 http://media.dissonantstates.com/i/EdgeUpright.jpg

I returned to the dressing room and munched numbly on a plum, then a pear, then an apple, then a yogurt, then a granola bar. Patty knocked on the door and stuck in her head. "Stress eating, dear?" I glanced at the pile of remains next to my gift basket. "Let me show you how we'll start the recital." I followed her into the dark backstage just behind the curtain, where she began to point out different cues. "Long story short, wait by the curtain, I'll dim the house lights from back there, and when they're completely off, you walk out." A gleam flashed in her eyes. "Stage lights up! Onto you!"

"Has anyone shown up?"

"Oh, yes. We probably have around sixty or so people." My audience was quite literally a significant fraction of Bigfork's population. "Small, but appreciative," she urged.

"Now what?" I said into the black vacuum where I assumed my audience sat. "Around the turn of the twentieth century, most composers asked themselves just that, and *American* composers in particular had an added burden. Their predecessors, for all intents and purposes, forged very little in terms of asserting a recognizable voice for American classical music, instead composing music that was often ambitious but caught up in the romantic language of their European idols. So when, in the early twentieth century, composers everywhere started forging their own individual musical languages, American composers found themselves, consciously or not, with the added responsibility to create new music in a way that would, for the first time ever, distinguish them as Americans. Each composer on tonight's program, I think, did that in his own unique way."

The piano sounded bad, but not as bad as I'd expected. The Ginastera sounded surprisingly at home on this percussive, clangy instrument, and the hollow, open intervals of the Copland pieces actually worked rather well with its tinny, slightly off-key tone. Every note on this piano had its own personality, a different tambour, even a different tuning, and it took only a few measures for me to realize that trying to impose any kind of uniformity upon its haphazard orchestra of eighty-eight keys would've caused more harm than good. Instead, I gave in, allowing the metallic twang here, the quarter-tone pitch there, and letting the cards fall where they may. After the show, I bowed to the black hole where my audience still seemed to remain, and returned backstage to my basket, starting immediately into a peach. Patty burst through the door. "ADAM!" she cried. "Wonderful!"

She brought me to the lobby. One patron called the program "so shocking it woke us up," adding, "we need that up here." Another woman demanded to see my music. "What a memory you have!" she said, leafing through the pages. It wasn't unusual for people to request a peak at my scores, so I usually came prepared with them. "I'd like to see you play some Mozart, though. *That's* what I like," she concluded, closing the books.

"You should get my CD, then," I answered. "It's over there, and only ten dollars."

BOZEMAN, MONTANA

The exit to Bozeman looks like every other exit on Interstate 90: industrial and unmemorable, with the usual gas stations and fast-food chains. Signs and arrows point visitors in the direction of Yellowstone Park while bright billboards advertise RV parks and campgrounds. Less than a mile down the road is the real Bozeman, rustic Bozeman, quaint Bozeman, college-town Bozeman, which, like any college town, seems blithely in love with itself and maintained to look precisely as it must have a hundred years ago. The same dark mountains I just drove through[46] with clenched teeth are reduced now to a harmless backdrop for beautiful girls in tank tops, sunglasses, and bright-colored sandals. Everyone looks tan and sexy, glowing with health and purpose.

I spot the Leaf and Bean, a coffee shop where I'll play my concert in two days. Its display window, with its countless posters of local artists who will soon play there, has no sign of my concert, but this is how it goes, I think to myself, because I'm not local, don't have a publicist, and don't even have a website. Inside, people chat at tables and work on laptops. On the far back wall I see the piano, another upright, on a slightly heightened stage. I remember that the manager of the shop claimed to have arranged a special tuning for my concert, and when I'd stressed in an email that the America 88x50 program wasn't exactly background music, she assured me that The Bean always had captive audiences for its concerts, and that she understood this was going to be a recital.

---

46 http://media.dissonantstates.com/i/MontanaHighway.jpg

On a chalkboard above the piano, just below *Tuesday: Bluegrass Jam*, it reads *Thursday: America 88x50*, and I like knowing that no customer to visit The Leaf and Bean this week can possibly have any idea what that means.

The International Backpacker's Hostel[47] is a small, discreet yellow house in a neighborhood not far from downtown. I walked inside, noticing couches of all colors, their cushions overflowing, books in every crevice, trail maps and bumper stickers tacked onto the walls, and a stereo softly playing the local college radio station. I checked in with a guy wearing wire-rimmed glasses and a spandex biking top, clutching a Tom Robbins book, and then collected my practice keyboard from the trunk and propped it up on a picnic table outside. Tapping away through technique drills, I started thinking about how in just over a month, mostly from the front seat of my car, I'd lined up about twenty-five states through September. But after that, I had nothing—glass half-empty—and though my project seemed like exactly the kind of thing that should've been attracting attention and gaining momentum, so far I'd gone relatively unnoticed, and the halfway mark of the tour seemed more like a brick wall with me bounding helplessly toward it in my Hyundai.

I could hear a little girl singing, dancing, and drifting along the sidewalk at the edge of the grass. She wore a one-piece sundress, and her long, unkempt dirty blonde hair kept falling to and fro as she howled her own little

47 http://dissonantstates.com/post/1027610854/montanafragment

improvised aria: "*I don't know what to doooooooo...I don't know...what...to doooooooooooo...*"

I was on the porch studying the yellow pages, looking for piano teachers whom I could call and invite to Thursday's concert—"And bring your students, too, please!"—when CJ, a young reporter passing through Bozeman doing research for a tourism company, stepped out to join me.

"So where are you from, and what are you doing?" she asked. I explained the project. "So, it's like a vacation," she said. I tried to clarify, explain it differently, maybe mention my mission of bringing American art music to communities who rarely get to hear it, or how America 88x50 was an experiment in grassroots arts outreach initiatives, to see if it was possible to execute a large-scale project without formal arts funding. But she was unmoved. "Sounds like a vacation."

"Well, I mean, I *guess* it's sort of like a vacation," I resigned.

"But I don't understand," she said, hunching forward. "Are you doing this as a kind of benefit, or are you trying to get discovered?"

I stumbled again into some new variation on the project's mission. "It's...um, it's...a statement against the norm imposed on independent artists that dictates they compromise..."

But she just looked at me. "I still don't really get it." And that was that. I remained quiet, hoping she would go away.

☆

The upright piano[48] was just feet away from the Leaf and Bean's restroom. I noticed this while stacking my music folder, an armful of newspapers, and two small phonebooks on a chair in front of the keyboard so I could reach the keys. Most of the people who'd gathered at the coffee shop tonight, and there were very few, had come with someone they wanted to chat with. They weren't here for me, and to introduce the concert cold from the stage into the chattering void seemed an ill choice. My heart sank. This scenario, happening right now, was exactly what I'd hoped to avoid. And here I had actually looked forward to this gig, to play for a coffee shop audience and get some kind of hip coffee shop reaction to the music. It could have been so cool.

Instead, it was coffee-grinders buzzing, blenders roaring, steamers hissing, ice buckets dumping, customers laughing, and employees shouting orders. Eager to get this over with, I turned my back on the shop and, without a word, sat facing the back wall (a small consolation) and slammed into that first interval of the Ives *Three-Page Sonata* with a severity that silenced the Leaf and Bean, if just for a moment, and played the rest of it with on-the-spot accuracy, the white-noise distraction of everyone else's activity and indifference forming a kind of protective membrane around me, just like in the Kansas City rug store. And, so protected, I tore into the rest of the program without restraint, like an animal, each note a retaliation against the toilet lid crashing down only feet away, the little boy screaming and sprinting between tables, the two men playing backgammon, the guy sound asleep in the rocking chair, the family reunion in the front of the store.

48 http://media.dissonantstates.com/i/BozemanUpright.jpg

When I glanced away from the piano, I saw the beginnings of a revolt, people shaking their heads, looking around for an explanation, as others streamed out in a huff. I was in the middle section[49] of the Griffes *Sonata*, a passage where simple Eastern melodies float over a dark sea of brooding chords, when a chorus of multiple blenders began, rendering me useless and, most shockingly, drowning out the squealing boy running between the tables who had, until now, more or less monopolized the spotlight. Perhaps surprised himself, he collided with one of these tables, sending a tumult of chairs and glasses showering in every direction. I wouldn't stop for an intermission. I had to keep going until the Copland *Sonata* closed the program, a moment significant this evening only because it coincided with a gargantuan smash of ice swooshed into a cooler from a bucket that was then dropped onto the floor, bouncing and thudding as I stepped down from the podium. A CD of folk music that had been playing when I arrived two hours earlier was immediately switched back on.

SANDPOINT, IDAHO

I'm in a concrete hut shaped like a fish head[50] on a lake shore in northern Idaho, roused by the sound of my own voice coming from a small, portable FM radio I've kept on all night beside my cot, my voice explaining America 88x50 in an in-studio interview I gave the day before to a

---

49 http://media.dissonantstates.com/a/GriffesSonataMiddleSection.mp3
50 http://media.dissonantstates.com/i/FishHeadCave.jpg

host at KPBX, a public radio station in Spokane. I wonder how many people are hearing me talk right now, and how many hours until my concert tonight, and how many days since I've practiced. I want to nestle back into this dusty green sleeping bag, but instead I prop myself up on my elbows and look through the hanging screen curtain that separates me from the lapping waves of the beach just a few feet away.

A sea monster[51] statue rises from the water, and a small island that I waded to yesterday, beautifully overgrown with trees and bushes, is just a few hundred feet offshore. This isolated fantasyland property was created by the presently absent brother of my Idaho concert host, Karen[52]. "He's a pirate," she'd answered, after some thought, when I asked what he did for a living. Statues and sculptures peek out from every corner, and his house emerges from the earth[53] like a petrified tree trunk. With him away, his property has fallen into the care of Jane, an artist and writer who lives quietly in an RV parked on the property, sharing her space with seven black rescue cats and writing a book about the lake. I see her coming around the side of my cave now with a cup of tea. She's very thin, with wiry brown hair and glasses. "Adam, you're on the radio! Are you hearing this?"

"I know!" I say, and swing my legs onto the sandy floor.

"I brought you some tea."

As she sits at the foot of the cot, I turn up the volume on my performance of Mozart's *Fantasy and Fugue in C*

---

51 http://media.dissonantstates.com/i/SeaMonster.jpg

52 http://dissonantstates.com/post/10070268863/balladofkaren

53 http://dissonantstates.com/post/3082988226/idaho#hobbit

Major K. 394[54] from my CD. The interview begins again. "I think I'm talking too much," I blurt out to Jane. "I sound pompous."

"It's an interview," she answers, staring at the crackling radio. "You're supposed to talk. And you don't sound pompous. You sound like the kind of person someone would want to be stuck on a deserted island with, just like he said." One of her black cats appears, sauntering between us and bumping headfirst into a leg of the cot. It has no eyes, a squashed nose, and a mouth displaced to where its cheek should have been. It's a Picasso, and its labored breathing hisses like a punctured bicycle tire. "A dog crushed his head," explains Jane, who notices me staring. "He's still such a sweet little cat, though, right? The dog was just trying to play."

From what I'd heard, Sandpoint had once enjoyed a kind of comfortable anonymity up here in the northernmost tip of Idaho's panhandle, a community of ex-hippies and perpetual beach bums poised at the seat of majestic Lake Pend Oreille and walled in by steep mountain peaks. It wasn't long before travel magazines discovered Sandpoint for all its hidden treasures and exposed it as one of the country's best-kept secrets. And so, as legend goes, wealthy out-of-staters, mostly Californians, began infiltrating the community with wrecking balls swinging and big plans for homes and strip malls, raising property taxes so dramatically that many longstanding

54 http://media.dissonantstates.com/a/MozartFantasyFugueCMajor.mp3

members of the community couldn't afford to stay. And perhaps this was a skewed narrative, but the day I arrived, what I believe was a mill tower near the center of town—a sign advertised it as "For Sale"—was targeted for demolition. Neglected, derelict, whatever the case, onlookers still wept openly as a machine began chewing away at the landmark's side. Cars unfortunate enough to bear California license plates had crept by the gruesome spectacle with caution, and one had a piece of paper shoved defensively onto the dashboard, a scrawled message that read: *I am a **RETURNING** local.*

Today, the morning of my recital, I passed by the pathetic heap of wooden planks where the tower once stood on my way to the Panida Theatre, another beloved community landmark that served as both a performing arts center and an art-house movie theater. The Panida would celebrate its twentieth anniversary with my America 88x50 concert, and I couldn't help but gaze in amazement at my name up there on the marquee[55]. I created this.

I handed the Panida's unenthused tech guy a few CDs of ambient electronic music by Aphex Twin and Moby to play before the show, another disc of more upbeat music for the intermission, and then rock music by The Kinks to be turned on the second I finished my John Adams encore[56]. I burned the CDs that morning in my fish-head cave, hoping to totally immerse my audience in an America 88x50 experience that wasn't limited to

55 http://media.dissonantstates.com/i/SandpointMarquee.jpg
56 http://media.dissonantstates.com/a/AdamsChinaGates.mp3

the genre of my program. I wanted my audience to feel like they were *part* of something, to engage them in the fantasy, the myth, the mystery I was consciously building about my tour and myself.

I'd envisioned my shows this way from the start, but had been too shy to suggest to my hosts that I have, at the very least, any pre-show, mid-show, or post-show music. But from now on I would insist on this element in every concert, even if it meant running backstage and pressing play and pause myself. By the time I was downstairs in a florescent-lit dressing room, I could hear the music playing. I watched the filling theater from a faded closed-circuit television screen[57].

Was the audience...? No, it couldn't be. I squinted, nearly pressing my face against the tiny screen. Yes. Virtually everyone had a bag of freshly popped popcorn. Others dug into small boxes of candy. And almost everyone sipped happily from straws pierced into the lids of paper soda cups. I laughed. This was wonderful. I wished I could serve popcorn to my audiences at every concert; at least they'd always have something to keep them happy and awake.

With the sight of the popcorn and the sound of the pre-show music, it was like I had Sandpoint's permission to now explode my piano recital into whatever I wanted it to be, and beyond that, my tour into whatever I dared to envision it as.

So tonight I'd start the show with something different. No more coming out on stage and talking before I played. I'd play first, and I'd play something that wasn't on the program. Yes, since Aphex Twin was playing over the

---

57 http://media.dissonantstates.com/i/ClosedCircuit.jpg

Panida's speakers at that very moment, I'd walk onstage and play the Aphex Twin piano tune[58] that I'd recently picked up off the electronic artist's album, *Drukqs*, while driving in the car, a solo piano track of such simplicity and beauty that I was able to transcribe it by ear from the CD. Sure, I knew Aphex Twin was a European artist with no ties whatsoever to my all-American program, but his small prelude would set the tone for my concert, I was sure, and starting tonight, I would kick off my shows with it, unannounced. I didn't know the song's title. It didn't matter.

LANDER, WYOMING

"Do you know the speed limit?"
   "Yes, actually. Forty-five. I just saw the sign."
   "No. Way back. Did you see the sign *way* back?"
   "Um…"
   "It said *fifty*-five."
   "Oh!…Well, that's good, then."
   "You were going eighty-five."
   "Ah…"
I could have sworn I was going a hundred. Still I begged, telling the officer about the wrong turn that sent me nearly an hour off course into Jackson Hole, and how I still had such a long way to go until Lander, my destination, and how none of this was an excuse for going so fast, but it just must have been the majesty of those Grand Tetons behind him, so captivating that I'd even stopped to take a picture[59] of my Hyundai—

---

58 http://media.dissonantstates.com/a/KessonDaslef.mp3
59 http://dissonantstates.com/post/3528206526/wyoming#tetons

"You got any alcohol in you to help you along the way? Any drugs?" He peered around me to the passenger seat, and then into the crowded trunk, packed as always to the hilt with the backseats down to accommodate my suitcases, music, and silent piano coffin.

"No!" I answered, mildly insulted, but also a lot more nervous; there's a certain powerlessness, a distinct vulnerability to telling the truth when you know someone doesn't want to believe you. I started to doubt even myself. *Was* I high? There was that mouthful of Excedrins I'd just crunched and swallowed, now coursing through my veins to quell a post-Yellowstone[60] headache. And then I considered the suitcase full of colitis meds in the back—enemas, suppositories, steroids, anti-inflammatories, immunosuppressants…

"You moving?" he asked, eyes still glued to the trunk. I told him about 88x50 and, just like the last cop I'd explained it to, he seemed delighted. It *did* sound cool to say I was on tour, I had to admit, even if I happened to leave out little facts like how I didn't know where I was sleeping that night or how in Sandpoint I'd given my contact info to a twelve-year-old girl vacationing with her family who said she could get me a show at her school back in Denver. "Well, let me go run your stuff and we'll see what we can do about this," the officer said. *What we can do about this.* That sounded promising. He returned to his car and I sat there staring into the rearview mirror. Minutes passed, many minutes, and then I saw him writing and staring at my license plate. Fuck. He was back at my window again. "So I only clocked you at eighty-two, but you were going eighty-five."

---

60 http://dissonantstates.com/post/3528206526/wyoming#yellowstone

"Excuse me?"

"Either way, it requires you to see the judge."

I began to sweat. My breath shortened. There was a good chance I might scream. And yet, there was also a weird lifting, because at least I knew where I was going to sleep that night. Jail could be interesting. "But, since you're moving around and I know you have stuff to do, I knocked it down to seventy-nine. So now you don't have to see the judge, but you still have a hefty fine. A hundred and twenty dollars." I'd made twice that in Bigfork alone. I offered to pay him right then and there, reaching into the middle console where I kept all my CD earnings; I had no bank to deposit it in. He declined. "But you have seven days to pay this, and if you don't, we'll have to put a nationwide warrant out on you. So that means you'll be wanted. Nationwide. You understand?"

"Yes." Inside, I smiled. Oh, to be wanted. Nationwide.

Lander seemed like the kind of town a tourist might stop in to rest awhile on his way someplace else. I, on the other hand, would be here for almost a week. It was around eleven p.m. After checking into the Silver Spur Motel, I drove back and forth through town, chasing fast-food closing times, missing each one by a minute, before finally stopping in a McDonald's parking lot and calling out to a group of employees smoking outside.

"Do you have *any* food? Anything!"

"We're closed," said a dark-haired woman. She cocked her head and squinted her eyes. "I think I saw your picture in the paper. You're a pianist, right?" Her short, gelled hair reflected the light of the golden arches. "Yeah, it's you. There's an article on you."

"Yes!" I shouted from my window, even though I didn't know what article she meant. "It's me! Nothing's open!"

"Do you have any CDs on you?" She leaned back and took a drag from her cigarette. "I love classical music."

"I have a whole box in the back," I said. "I'm playing Mozart, Brahms, Hindem—"

"I'll trade you one for an apple pie."

It was a deal. She flicked her cigarette and walked back into the McDonald's as I dug behind my passenger seat for the box of discs. When she emerged with not one, but six apple pies, I grabbed more CDs and handed them out to everyone. "We'll listen as we close," she said as they all disappeared. I wanted to invite them to my concert that Friday but realized I didn't remember where it would take place. I hadn't read the article[61].

Life in the Silver Spur: I bake for a week amidst sunburned furniture, practicing on my silent keyboard, watching competitive eating tournaments and trashy talk shows on a prehistoric television, and harassing no-response venues, trying to cultivate *something* in the Midwest, the Deep South, the Northeast—anywhere.

---

61 http://media.dissonantstates.com/i/LanderArticle.jpg

The Carnegie Room[62] of the Freemont County Library has dark red carpeting, a chandelier, a fireplace, and over a hundred folding chairs set up by my host, Marvin[63]. An older man from another generation, he refers to my concert as an "act."

"So when's your act?" he asks, glancing at his watch as we sit alone before the piano.

He should know; he set up my show. "Seven-thirty," I answer. "Ten minutes."

"People 'round here always come *right* before the show," he says. "Don't worry."

And yes, at 7:28, people start trickling in. I personally greet each one, noting that most are around his age—I'd guess in their seventies. A woman brushes past me and snaps, "I couldn't get in through the front door!" She's the last person to arrive. The weight of the rest of the tour hits me with a sudden, exhausting force, the reality that I'm going to do this thirty-seven more times after tonight, and at once I feel immeasurably far from where I started, a kitchen table in Vermont with my atlas, and yet also like I've gone almost nowhere at all. Like this—playing a Wyoming library for an audience of twelve, where I was just mistaken for an usher—is as far as America 88x50 will ever go.

RATON, NEW MEXICO

A high rock face towered over the city with the word RATON dancing across it in huge white letters like the

---

62 http://media.dissonantstates.com/i/CarnegieRoom.jpg
63 http://dissonantstates.com/post/10136227857/balladofmarvin

Hollywood sign—"rat" in Spanish—overlooking this town, old but not really charming, quiet but not really pleasant, as if for the past fifty years no one felt the need to dust the jewelry store display windows or change the pictures on the diner walls.

But the Shuler Theatre was a different story. Bart, its director, met me outside and led me in. Short, wide, and leaning forward, with a few strands of white hair clinging to his perfectly round head, Bart brought me to center stage before retreating into the darkness behind the curtains. I took a quick picture of the piano[64] before spinning around slowly, taking it all in, the ornately carved walls that climbed and reached for the ceiling which itself was framed in gold with a painting of the sky in the middle, a painting so vibrant and blue, with electric colors and wispy clouds, that it seemed almost like a perfect window to a perfect day. "It's beautiful," I said to Bart, wherever he was.

When Bart said yes to America 88x50, he told me he was also a booking agent, so I especially looked forward to meeting him today and making, I hoped, a good enough impression that he might help me book some future shows. After showing me the Shuler, he took me to a quiet restaurant a few miles away, a kind of Howard Johnson's. Bart was friendly and well known among the patrons inside, and he diligently plugged America 88x50 to each person who greeted him. "Many of these people already know about you," he said, motioning around the room once we sat and ordered, "because I've told them."

"And thanks so much for that," I said. "You know I need it."

---

64 http://media.dissonantstates.com/i/ShulerPiano.jpg

"Let me know when you're playing again around the Great Lakes area and I'll tell my agent friends there." Here it was, the moment I'd been waiting for. "They can come and see you play, maybe line up some recitals. They already have their pianist for the season, but maybe they could add you on in the future if they like you."

If they like me? This sounded like an audition, and just thirteen concerts into the tour, I'd already grown used to playing my own recitals on my own terms, calling myself a pianist and being let in the door. Auditioning, from my experience, meant failing. I never wanted to do it again. I wanted to keep living whatever masquerade this was, because in a lot of ways it was working. Perhaps Bart saw the pallor of my face change. "They just book you shows," he said gruffly, digging into his catfish. "They won't manage you. They just get you concerts so you don't have to do all the scrambling you're doing now. Since we've met, you haven't let go of that phone." He was staring into his plate as he spoke, but wagging a greasy butter knife in my direction. "See, if you had an agent, you could spend your time *practicing* instead of being on the phone."

He was right.

But inside I felt I wasn't ready for an agent. Even if I had the brains and the chops, and maybe I had both, there simply wasn't enough time for me to catch up on the same standard repertoire that virtuoso concert pianists had in their fingers since diapers, since their competition days. I played tough-as-nails music, but was no virtuoso. I learned that at IU if I learned anything at all. And while I knew I wouldn't spend the rest of my life chasing that dream or that music, I still knew I had something to say, a place in music, even if there wasn't a platform, let alone an agent alive, for a pianist like me. That was the point of America 88x50, or at least one of them—to create that platform.

At least today it was, right now, talking to Bart. Tomorrow it could be something else. It wasn't so much about getting discovered, as CJ in Bozeman had posited, as it was about learning to play the piano without having to stay in school, playing for people without asking permission, being an artist without having to audition. CJ didn't get it then, and I wasn't sure Bart would get it now. So I changed the subject. "I'm thinking of taking 412 from New Mexico across the Oklahoma panhandle to get to my next show in Tulsa," I said. "That way, instead of dipping south on I-25 to hook onto I-40 just to go all the way back north again, I can go straight across. And it'll be more scenic, right?"

Bart shook his head, chewing as he answered, still looking at his plate. "You obviously have no idea what you're doing."

She places the phone on her shoulder, looks up from her seat, and asks me point blank how much longer the program will last. "The second part is a little shorter than the first," I say. "Maybe thirty-five, forty minutes?" But I want to ask why she needs to know. Where's she going? Who does she need to see? I want to admonish her for having the nerve to ask me, the performer, how much longer I'll be playing! Outrageous.

"Oh, okay," she answers with a smile. "I'm calling some friends to tell them to come. One sec." She guards the receiver with her free hand and directs her attention back to the caller. "He says about thirty-five, forty minutes. *You have time! Come!*"

A man appears in front of me, a carpenter maybe, because he wears a dusty plaid shirt and has a tape measure hanging from his belt. He gives me a firm handshake and instructs his son, hiding behind his kneecaps, to do the same. I ask if he has any WD-40 for me to spray on the piano's squeaking pedal and he lights up, pleased, it seems, that I even know what WD-40 is. And I, likewise, am pleased to find out that Alberto Ginastera is one of his favorite composers.

At Denny's after the show, I watched a young Mexican girl standing before an arcade machine filled with stuffed animals as her father fed handfuls of quarters to the machine, manipulating a mechanical claw inside, trying to win her a prize. Again and again, the claw lowered, swiped halfheartedly at the toys, and then rose empty, until he had no more quarters left. When they left, I pushed away my dish, no longer hungry.

Bart had a small ranch house on a narrow dirt road outside Raton. Like Raton, it may have needed an update. My feet sank into his dark shag carpet, and statues, pillows, magazines, and books lay in stacks on the floor. As Bart disappeared into his room, I stood in the living room and thumbed through one of his books, *Gays In Hollywood*, a hardcover I was nervous he'd see me with since he might ask me why I was so interested. Bart called from the bedroom and I closed the book with a start.

"My bed is a Magic Fingers." I put the book down and poked my head down the hallway to look into his bedroom; he was already in his undershirt and boxers, but facing the other direction. "Magic Fingers is a vibrating bed," he explained, walking out of sight again. "And you can share it with me if you want. I promise I won't molest you."

Assuring as that was, I said no. He shut off the light, turned on the bed, and the house began to shake.

Bart seemed so alone out here, living in a house he shared only with his books and souvenirs of the past. Whether or not these days I was just digging in my heels as best I could, as gravity and age and exhaustion pulled me closer to acknowledging the obvious, this seemed to be where it all led: a ranch house on the outskirts of Raton, alone with a Magic Fingers bed. Suddenly I had my doubts that it was so heroic to be honest with oneself after all.

Maybe it went both ways. Maybe I reminded Bart of an earlier time in his life, an unhappier, less honest time. Maybe he wanted to free me from a jail he recognized, a jail he'd once also inhabited. Maybe I frustrated him for more reasons than my proposed route to Tulsa. Maybe he wanted to shake some sense into me, or at least shake me into a stronger sense of identity, with his Magic Fingers bed.

He left the next morning before I woke up, leaving a note.

One of The Shuler's never-married, solemn support-
ers has covered, as I expected, the concert's expenses,
although he hated everything you played. He admired
your pianism, however, and said if you ever came back
with a "traditional program" he'd support it finan-
cially. He even suggested that you might someday have
a piano trio on tour. How about an all-male trio? Most
of the young classical groups we've toured in the past few
years have been made up of Asian girls. They play won-
derfully, of course, but an all-male, young trio would be
somewhat of a novelty—now isn't that a change?

Love—Bart

TULSA, OKLAHOMA

"What are you listening to?" I asked Aaron, an administrator at the Barthelmes Conservatory, as he bustled
around the office. "Is it children's music?" I was gazing
at an article[65] about my upcoming concert that he'd
handed me, and that he'd single-handedly generated.

"You don't know?" he asked, suddenly immobilized.
"This is *Oklahoma!* This is what we're taking you to see
tonight."

"Excuse me?"

"It's tradition." He pushed a brochure in my
direction: *Discoveryland! National Home of Rodgers and
Hammerstein's Oklahoma!* "Unless you're too tired."

I'd taken the scenic route to Tulsa after all, at one
point driving on five highways at once[66], through long

---

65 http://media.dissonantstates.com/i/TulsaArticle.jpg

66 http://media.dissonantstates.com/i/OklahomaRoutes.jpg

desert expanses littered only with the shells of ancient service stations[67] and long-dead motels[68]. I'd pulled off the highway and urinated in the foundation of one, staring through the peeling, wafer-thin walls and wondering what might have once been there, what memories were now escaping out into the open air. But I wasn't tired. In fact, I was getting kind of used to this lifestyle, these long drives.

Discoveryland! didn't have the roller coasters and clowns I expected. It was actually rather subdued, not much more than an outdoor park with a subtle frontier theme, whose main function appeared to be hosting summer musicals in its outdoor amphitheater. Men on horses galloped by, kicking up golden dust, and one gave a small group of onlookers a demonstration of the Pony Express, grabbing a letter from a young man, riding his horse into the distance, and then turning around and coming back.

At the amphitheater, Aaron surveyed the red plastic seats, bolted permanently into the concrete. He appeared pleased. "They changed the seats." We walked to the third row. The set was elaborate, houses built alongside onstage trees and hills of dirt and grass. I was actually getting excited and looked around at my fellow audience of, what, fifty people? Well, it was a Wednesday. "Where's the orchestra?" I asked, sitting up to look for the hidden ensemble.

"It's a CD."

"Howdy, y'all!" shouted a voice. I jumped in my seat. There was a young man in a cowboy outfit moseying

---

67 http://media.dissonantstates.com/i/ServiceStation.jpg

68 http://media.dissonantstates.com/i/GhostMotel.jpg

toward a microphone placed in the middle of the stage. Some people greeted him back. "Before the show," he continued in an exaggerated twang, "we'd like to give you a brief review of the history of America!" My eyes widened. "...And the history of this fine state of Oklahoma...*through song!* We want to show y'all what it means *to be an American!*"

Aaron leaned toward me and whispered, "They might do a tribute to 9/11."

Before I could even imagine how to reply, dozens of costumed cast members flanked the stage, lining up beside the young man as country music blasted from amplifiers placed in the trees of the set. They stamped their feet in unison, swayed their bodies, and held their hands up high like showgirls. The song wasn't an elegy to 9/11, nor from what I could tell a tribute to any kind of history of America or Oklahoma, but rather an ode to Discoveryland! And when it changed to a new song, a new group made their way to the stage. The first bunch fell into the background and observed their successors with gazes of fascination, the men hanging on their knees, resting their chins in their hands, and the ladies with their legs crossed, regarding each other.

"*Shoulda' been a cowboy!*" a man belted into the microphone as the cast square-danced around him, and when this abridged version of Toby Keith's country anthem finished, he began to speak, saying something along the lines of "...Gonna give y'all a chance to come up here and dance with us..." Audience participation? As people were led onto the stage, I began planning an escape route, maybe to a restroom where I'd hide in a stall until it seemed safe to reemerge. And just as I readied myself, the music cut silent with a deadened electric thud. The cast scurried, almost running for their lives, offstage and into the shadows of the set, leaving the few unfortunate audience members who had volunteered to dance with them abandoned onstage like deserted prom dates.

"Does it always end like that?" I asked Aaron.

"I think someone may have tripped over a chord."

Moments later, a frumpy un-costumed employee appeared and informed us that Discoveryland! had lost all power and an electrician was on the way, and that if the show was cancelled, we would all receive vouchers for a free show. "Within the next five years," he clarified. We sat for forty-five minutes before getting an answer. Vouchers, it was! Aaron was visibly crestfallen. "It's fine!" I assured him. "Now you can bring someone else here for free! I don't care! I had fun." He just shook his head.

The cast returned to the stage, and the emcee, speaking on their behalf, reassured us that everyone felt terrible for the night's events and didn't want us to leave without hearing the title song of *Oklahoma!* One of the female cast members stepped forward, turned to her cast mates, hummed the first note, and everyone commenced perfectly into an a cappella rendition of the song. Their voices echoed through the trees and reverberated against the speakers that hung dormant in the canopy above them. The audience clapped along as the cast beat their knees and danced through the choreography. They no longer looked like showgirls, and for the first time I believed their smiles. The song ended to thunderous applause from our humble audience, and it occurred to me that the emcee in the cowboy outfit had actually kept his promise. In a way, the cast did show us all what it meant to be American.

There was such an influx of people who entered during my concert's intermission that I had to ask, once the recital ended, where everyone had come from. One woman told me she'd heard the evening re-broadcast of my interview[69] from that morning on Tulsa Public Radio. "I was washing the dishes from dinner and then just had to drop everything to come straight here. I think everyone else must've heard the interview too."

Just then, a tall, balding man came between us, his eyes furious. "You *are* a professional," he said, nearly shouting. "Don't *ever* doubt that. You *are* a professional." I didn't know what to say. It was like he had read my mind, discovered my doubts hidden somewhere. But how? I thanked him and turned to sign an autograph.

LEXINGTON, KENTUCKY

On my way to Kentucky, I stopped at a gas station somewhere in southern Illinois to fill up the tank. Barely noticing the small town I'd stopped in, I turned on the pump and ran inside to use the bathroom. I came out of the little room at the back of the store a few minutes later to find the attendant, an older woman with her hair in a bun, calmly pointing from behind the cash register out the window toward my Hyundai, sitting in

69 http://media.dissonantstates.com/a/TulsaInterview.mp3

a lake of gasoline, the tank and nozzle overflowing in a spectacular shower of fuel in all directions.

"WHY DIDN'T IT TURN OFF?" I shouted, bolting to the glass door. Then, as I tore it open, "WHY DIDN'T *YOU* TURN IT OFF!" And then, sprinting toward the fountaining spectacle, "JESUS, TURN IT OFF!!" Several townspeople were already running to the scene with buckets of soapy water and large brushes. I pulled the dripping nozzle from the tank and placed it back in its harness, glancing at my purchase total, over seventy dollars. *Please Stay at the Pump While Filling,* a sign read. *We Are Not Responsible for Spills.* I needed to get out of there. Wading through the pool of gasoline to my driver's side door, I waved obliviously to the panicked cleanup crew— "Thanks, guys!"—and lowered myself into the car, sneakers and cuffs soaked. Holding my breath, I turned the key as a headline flashed across my mind: PIANIST PERISHES IN GAS STATION DISASTER. TOWN LEVELED. But the car started without detonating, and I pulled out slowly, gas dripping from my tires and trailing behind me. I watched as the crowd and the mess and whatever authorities were on their way shrank in the rearview mirror.

This seemed to sum up my relationship with the places and people of America 88x50. I'd sweep in for a couple minutes, briefly skirt disaster, and then disappear with a few souls temporarily affected, for better or worse.

As for Kentucky, my concert would serve all of three people of Lexington. The three women sat in the front row, muttering niceties. "Our own private concert…"

I approached the piano, a Boston baby grand piano standing alone[70] and embarrassed in the middle of

---

70 http://media.dissonantstates.com/i/LexingtonPiano.jpg

the stark gallery. "I think we're going to start now," I interrupted with a whisper, and they sat up. After Ives's *Three-Page Sonata*, one of the women—she had short hair and wore an aqua shawl—raised her hand as if she was in a classroom. This was a first. I pointed at her like a schoolteacher. "Yes?"

"So angry," she stated, frowning. "I sense anger."[71]

One of the women, Helene, gave me a ride after the concert to a small upscale restaurant a few blocks from the gallery. On the way, she described her work as an abstract painter and said that she'd connected with the music of my program, particularly the Copland, and this surprised her. "I listened to Copland once and—I don't know what it was—but I just said, 'This isn't for me.' And I never cared to listen to him again. But something about tonight and what you played. It was tender, yet jagged. I suddenly *heard* it," she said, clasping her hands over the steering wheel. "I heard *him*."

"I'm glad you were there," I said. "Like, when nobody— I mean, when just a *few* people show up, there's a different energy to the show. An intimacy."

"Well, the right people were there," she said.

"That's true."

"You know, I love nights like this! I got an e-mail from the gallery this afternoon, invited my two friends, and now here we are after a surprise concert of totally enlightening music, and going to a dinner!"

---

71 http://dissonantstates.com/post/10985803422/a-note-on-ives

We joined Helene's two other friends and Jim, the executive director of ArtSpace, at a round table outside the restaurant. Jim, with wine, had melted from the stoic man I'd briefly met at the gallery into a colorful prankster who could momentarily entertain one subject before starting into another two seconds later. *Gay*, I told myself. *He was definitely gay*. It still was so exotic and foreign—the idea that someone could be out of the closet. What was it like? How did it feel to be Jim? Was it the same as how it felt to be Bart in Raton? Or Michael in Spencer? Or Bruce in Kansas City? How did it feel?

A car thumped by, its bass rattling our silverware. Over the music, Helene tried to address the table, nearly shouting. "Do you remember when that woman went to court for playing her car stereo too loud, and the judge sentenced her to a year without music in her car?"

"Only in Kentucky," Jim laughed.

Helene mused, "That guy in the car, making us all listen to his music, is he doing it as a performance? Is that his self-expression? Or is it a power thing?"

"Yes," interjected Jim brusquely. "It's a power thing. Only someone who has no power over anything in their life forces other people to listen to their music."

I gulped. Just then, a fountain shot up in front of what looked like a courthouse. Even though it was late, children appeared and began dashing through the fountain as colored lights flashed.

"They wanted to put a very abstract sculpture there but the city said, 'No way!'" Helene said, turning around to see what had distracted me. "So they put in those fountains and it's become a real hit." She slumped a little in her chair, her gaze returning to the table. "Water's always nice."

"That's an art piece right in front of it," her short-haired friend said, pointing.

I squinted. "What? The newspaper stands?"

Before she could answer, Jim put another revelation to the table. "You play the piano with your sex chi, Adam. Did they teach you that at Indiana? Or did you, uh…pick that up out here on the road?"

I nearly choked on my wine. "I use…I need my whole body to play."

"This isn't politics, dear," he vamped. "We're all friends here!"

"Adam's shy," Helene purred, "Though I can't imagine what anyone would need to be shy about at age twenty-three."

I scanned my memory for examples. The Vermont forest with that tattooed cop? The baseball dugout with Calv—

"He doesn't need to tell you anything!" Jim laughed. "You get a play-by-play of it by just watching him at the piano!" The table erupted into laughter, almost seeming to toast the idea. "No, seriously, Adam," he said, suddenly quiet and piercing me with a glare I didn't yet know he was capable of. "You don't have a closet. You have a vault."

Our eyes were locked, and in the space of a breath, the only sound in Lexington, nearly imperceptible, was that of each lady at the table swallowing her wine.

EASTON, MARYLAND

The charms of Easton—its ocean air, its shops and restaurants, the bed and breakfast where I was staying

(I had the master wedding suite)—all crumbled into a formless history when I sat at the grand piano on the stage of the Avalon Theatre, probably one of the most prestigious venues I'd play in this entire tour. They'd advertised, promoted, even hired a photographer from the paper[72]—and no one was here. Again.

After the show, I walked up a set of stairs backstage to retrieve some of my things from the offices above the theater, passing sheets of paper taped to the walls carrying messages—for actors, I supposed—in big bold lettering: REACT! REACT! REACT! REACT! BE EXCITING! BE ENGAGING! BE REAL! BE YOU! Once upstairs, a young man in glasses saw me and apologized for the small turnout. "Some advertising fuck-up," he said. "My fault."

I told him it was fine, and quoted Helene from Lexington: "The right people were there." However, I couldn't help but think that one of those "right people" sneezed twice on the final *pppp* note of the Copland *Sonata*, the final note of the program.

MILFORD, DELAWARE

The Causey Mansion[73], now a bed and breakfast, was built in 1763, predating the Declaration of Independence, and Ken and Fran, the quintessential grandma and grandpa couple, ran it with pride. "That garage across the driveway was the slave quarters[74]," said Fran, pointing

---

72 http://media.dissonantstates.com/i/AvalonNewspaper.jpg

73 http://media.dissonantstates.com/i/CauseyMansion.jpg

74 http://media.dissonantstates.com/i/SlaveQuartersCameraGlitch.jpg

across the table and out the screen door. I'd just arrived
to a breakfast of fruit and eggs. "We'd love to hear some
of your stories from the road!"

"So you're playing *Burl* Ives?" Ken interjected, grinning. "Or am I in the wrong crowd here?" A knock came
from the kitchen door and Liz let herself in. The director of the Delaware Music School, a small community
school not unlike Barthelmes in Tulsa; she wore a flow-
ery blouse, slacks, and black-rimmed glasses.

"We expected you sooner," Fran said with a smile.

"Be nice to me, Fran. I just gave blood." Liz pointed
to a sticker on her shirt, then turned to me, her tone
sunny. "So nice to meet you! How's the tour going? You
must be dead tired." She shook my hand and helped
herself to some fruit. "I'd like to show you the school.
It's only a block or so away."

When we opened the door to leave, a gust of heat
from outside blasted the kitchen like an open oven
door, and as Liz and I strolled down the driveway my legs
had already begun to bake inside my jeans. She spoke of
Milford[75] like a kind of beloved work-in-progress, something that once was, something that used to be, but also
something that could be revived into something beautiful once again with the right amount of dedication and
work.

"When I came here the whole downtown was
boarded up," Liz said. "All the work and business
moved from downtown out toward the highway. But
slowly people have started to renovate and fix things
up." We approached a gigantic abandoned theater[76].

75 http://media.dissonantstates.com/i/MilfordTower.jpg

76 http://media.dissonantstates.com/i/MilfordTheatre.jpg

"And then you have this thing." Liz stopped. "The whole town wants to clean it up and get it functioning again, but at this point it would cost at least a million dollars. It has a lot of exterior damage and I guess the inside is moldy and decaying. But look at this outside, this marquee!" I'd never seen anything so majestic and yet so forlorn, a standing corpse of a building, with faded neon lights and empty poster slots. That is, except for one poster that read JESUS LORD JESUS LOVES YOU[77]. "Everything's there, though," she said with a small trace of optimism. "Intact, I mean. There's still a balcony, a stage, everything. It's *huge*. But the inside is just…" She couldn't finish, just shook her head. We walked on. "And here's the school."

In the window, I noticed a large poster: *Adam Tendeler presents America 88x50*[78]. I didn't have the heart to tell Liz that this display and, as I would later discover, all the programs and promotional materials, had my name misspelled. It would ruin her morning. She'd given blood.

Inside, the walls were pure white and the carpet smelled new. Some men were installing a new front door, which thrilled Liz. Hanging on the walls were photographs of smiling students with instruments, and I passed several teaching studios with upright pianos. "You'll play back here tonight," she said, leading me into a small banquet area flooded with florescent light and scattered with folding metal chairs and a brown Kawai grand piano[79].

---

77 http://media.dissonantstates.com/i/JesusSaves.jpg

78 http://media.dissonantstates.com/i/Tendeler.jpg

79 http://media.dissonantstates.com/i/DelawarePiano.jpg

Liz confessed that she'd only recently taken the position as the school's executive director, and that it had actually fallen so deeply into debt that, if they didn't meet their student enrollment goal this year, it could and probably would close. I thought of all those pictures of the grinning kids with their instruments. I thought of that decrepit theater down the road.

It was maybe six hours later when one of the music school's administrators burst into the teaching studio where I was warming up. "We need to make more programs! We have more people than programs!"

"That's great!" I said, standing up and following him out into the main office area.

"Liz is introducing you now," he said as paper churned out from the printer. "I'll hand these out by the time you start. Go! Go!" A minute later, he had, indeed, already handed out programs to the people who needed them. The audience was clapping and Liz received me with a hug and a whisper: "Thank you so much."

After the concert[80], once the school had emptied, Liz was folding chairs and rearranging the room as I counted CD money. $310...$320...$330...

"Honestly, I never thought we'd fill the house!" she was saying. "And there was one woman who came tonight who, in the early days, was really instrumental

---

80 http://dissonantstates.com/post/11068177117/delawarefragment

to the school's development. That is, before she left. But tonight she was *here!* And she told me she plans to return to the school. She loved your concert. She loved *you!* And she also knows the trouble we're in, so she could bring in a lot of money. It's *so* important that she came tonight. She met you afterwards, remember?"

$370...$380...$390...

"Well, it doesn't matter anyway. You met so many people. The point is that she came, and her change of heart might just save the school."

$410! I looked up smiling. "It's really amazing!"

CHAMBERSBURG, PENNSYLVANIA

He finally says it. He wants to meet. The message appears in an instant message on my computer screen after hours of preamble. It's late, after midnight, and the remnants of my dinner are cold and unrecognizable in a crumpled McDonald's bag on the floor, exuding the faint odor of American cheese and ketchup. He says he'll be at a bar somewhere between my Days Inn and Gettysburg.

It seems I've slowly graduated from straight porn to straight *guys*—finding them in chat rooms, exchanging messages for a few hours and extracting confessions from these farmers and jocks and husbands and fathers in the hollow blue light of the computer screen. It's a game, I suppose, because either I capture my prey or he disappears. This sudden and secret intimacy gives the exchange its own kind of honesty—a fantasy shared, and therefore a fantasy made real.

But rarely does it escalate to him dutifully describing the car he'll be driving to the bar and the clothes he'll wear. My stomach turns, a moment of clarity in the heat of courtship, and I think, *So this is the best I can do, wrapped in the luxury of isolation and anonymity out here in America?* Shame compounds upon shame, because it's not even so much my own cowardice to accept who—or what—I am, but my impotence, my fear, my laziness to act upon it even in the most protected and clandestine of opportunities. Like now. To move past sitting on my ass drooling like a fool while staring at the laptop, when I could be out *there*. Out there doing it! No, I realize, I'm not even a good closet case.

I look toward my folder of music. If only I devoted the same energy I give to my capricious online sex life to my music, to my tour…

And then I float out of the room and to the car, starting toward Gettysburg. I'm going to do it! Lonely acoustic folk music accompanies my drive, and when I arrive, I immediately recognize the car he described. Pins of adrenaline prick across my body. People outside the club watch as my Hyundai weaves slowly through the parking lot, creeping along in that unmistakable pace of the lost. But I'm not lost. And I'm also not stopping. It's like the fear of whatever, whomever, I'm here to meet has me magnetically opposed to parking the car. And all this mingles with a tantalizing excitement dancing around inside, the idea that I could be doing something bad out here in rural Pennsylvania that no one would ever know about.

Without further hesitation, I drive out of the parking lot and back toward the Days Inn. This is me in the unadulterated backyard of America 88x50. Driving away.

☆

Andrew and I started off on the wrong foot, and it probably started all the way back when I first proposed the concert to his Cumberland School of Music and he asked me to send a CD so he could, as he said, see if I "could really play." With that eventually out of the way—apparently, I could—we set the date for August 15, and he warned in an e-mail that I better not flake on the commitment. A month earlier I called Cumberland from Iowa to confirm the concert and see if they needed any additional materials besides my ever-developing press release—a mish-mash of other people's articles that I e-mailed presenters. The secretary I spoke to said she saw the concert right there in the calendar and didn't need anything but the release. All this made for a shock when, a few days ago in Easton, an e-mail arrived from Andrew with the subject: "Chambersburg Performance Cancelled." In the e-mail he scolded me for having not communicated with the school to confirm the date and for never sending a press release. I called and the same secretary answered. "What happened?" I'd asked. "I called over a month ago and you said it was all set. Do you remember? I'm on my way to Chambersburg as we speak!"

"Well, Andrew isn't here right now. I mean, he's *here*...but not in his office."

"What does that mean? He sent me an e-mail five minutes ago."

"You could leave him a message," she suggested.

"All right."

There was a long silence.

"We don't have voicemail. You'll have to just tell me the message."

"Oh. Okay…" I gathered myself. "Tell him that I called a month ago and spoke with you, and that you confirmed the date and said it was in the calendar. And then you can tell him that I e-mailed a press release to him personally when *he* confirmed the concert. And then you can tell him that I'll see all of you in a couple da—"

"He's here right now," she interrupted. "Hold on. You can tell him yourself."

I was suddenly uneasy, nervous, shrinking inside. There was some muffled dialogue and then his voice. "Hey Adam. So sorry. They just told me about you calling."

"And I sent you a press release!" I cried, feeling a new burst of energy.

"I don't know what happened, and at this point I just don't think we can get you an audience. It's so close to the concert."

"Well, I don't know what to tell you, but…" I took a breath, "I have to perform this show. We have a couple days. Call the paper and print some posters."

When I arrived from the Days Inn at Cumberland Valley School of Music, I saw a newspaper article[81]—one of two[82] that appeared in local papers that week—about the tour photocopied onto 8x11 paper and taped to the walls, windows, and doors with highlighter streaked over the important details. Andrew had, in a way, pulled

---

81 http://media.dissonantstates.com/i/ChambersburgArticle.jpg

82 http://media.dissonantstates.com/i/ChambersburgArticle2.jpg

through. The performance would take place in a large, bright auditorium with a dome over the stage. It was a chapel, but instead of pews there were comfortably padded theater seats. There was no air conditioning, but rather a huge fan that stood at the foot of the stage. It was probably ninety degrees in the hall before the audience had even arrived. This was an athletic program, to say the least, so I had a difficult choice in my future: turn the fan off and turn my concert hall into a sweatbox, or keep it on and struggle to hear my own playing?

The piano[83], a Steinway, nine feet long, waited at center stage, lid open. I turned it slightly so that people could see my hands if they wanted. I sat and reviewed my repertoire, playing it slow and calculated, listening close, listening deep, wanting to connect with my sound beyond the keyboard, like I was extending my ear to the far end of the strings.

About twenty people showed up, most of them elderly, with one twenty-something guy sitting alone in the balcony. It occurred to me, as I saw so many grey-haired people in the audience, that the elderly had time and again proved remarkably loyal to my concerts. It wasn't as simple as the generalization that old folks "just go" to classical concerts. Even if it were true, that stereotype, the music of my concert was far from *classical*, and anyone remotely versed in classical music would know that. No, the implications here were of something far better; these people took chances on their local arts offerings, scouring the paper for off-the-beaten-path (and sure, maybe free) events, and then—gasp!—they'd actually go! It was an astonishingly ballsy recreational activity, coming to an

---

83 http://media.dissonantstates.com/i/ChambersburgPiano.jpg

America 88x50 recital, and one that elderly audiences routinely accomplished, while my own hipper-than-thou demographic of twenty-somethings could scarcely ever be found in attendance. Even the young man sitting in the balcony left halfway through the concert[84].

☆

"All this from donations? And only one person bought a CD?" I asked Andrew, sitting at his desk as I held the heavy cardboard box of CDs against my body. My armpits reeked and sweat was pooling through my tight black performance shirt.

Andrew looked up. "I think people would have bought more CDs if they had tonight's program on them."

"You're probably right."

"*I'd* want a recording of tonight's program," he said, almost to himself. "Oh!" Andrew seemed disrupted by a new thought. "So if you're staying in the dorm tonight[85], I need those twenty-two dollars from you. Sorry about all the confusion about yesterday or whatever, with you having to find a motel. Did you get any sleep at the Days Inn?"

"A little," I said, shuffling through my wallet.

"We'd love to have you back," he said.

I nodded, still looking down. "Yeah." Twenty dollars to stay in a dorm? It seemed crazy.

"You inspired me tonight. You should know that."

Then I looked up.

"I, uh…" he leaned back in his office chair, "I really need to get on the ball again with my own composing.

---

84 http://dissonantstates.com/post/4826686356/pennsylvania#concert

85 http://dissonantstates.com/post/4826686356/pennsylvania#dorm

Life got so busy. I just let it go. I needed to see a young person like you just traveling and doing what you have to do to play. And you do it because it's what you love. I need to do the same thing."

I was completely still, staring at him, almost hypnotized, hand still in my wallet.

"It was everywhere, tonight, that feeling. I heard one woman say to her husband—and I *know* them, mind you, he's an artist and she, well, I don't know what she does—but she said, 'Babe, *you* could do that!' She said it over and over."

I was quiet. My body shivered, eyes welling. "I don't feel inspiring." The words came out of me almost without permission. They were so true it hurt. But at least they were out.

"Why? Are you used to making more money?"

I realized that Andrew's eyes were focused on the wallet still frozen in my hands. "No, no! It's not that..." I said, shaking myself back into the moment.

"You might've made more if you hadn't turned off that fan."

NASHVILLE, NORTH CAROLINA

A sequence of torrential downpours led to two gargantuan wrecks[86] on I-70 and I-95, respectively. At the latter standstill, I exited my car—the odometer having hovered for an hour at 14,999[87]—and peed off the bank of the interstate, returning to my car both completely

---

86 http://media.dissonantstates.com/i/AccidentAhead.jpg
87 http://media.dissonantstates.com/i/14999.jpg

relieved and not a bit affected by the consternated looks
of my fellow roadmates. An hour later, a generous man
in a Taurus saved me from what would've certainly been
hours more in traffic simply by warning me from his
window not to merge into a certain highway lane that I
was drifting toward in the glacial flow of cars. "All those
lanes are closed!" he yelled, his prescience unexplained.
I followed him onto a feeder road where we glided by
miles of stopped vehicles[88], drivers standing outside of
their car doors, pacing desperately, peeing freely over
the guardrail.

Eventually I saw it—a thrashing snapshot of destruction; one gigantic tractor-trailer entangled with several
unrecognizably twisted cars. My breath stolen, my mind
calculating the body count, I still cruised past with a
certain sense of gratitude for my psychic guide in his
Taurus, and waved in thanks as we merged back onto
the clear interstate. Onward.

In Nashville, the buildings looked miniature, the
stores quaint, the people friendly. Even with the typical generic fortress of fast-food chains, gas stations,
and box stores near the highway, the town itself had
retained a kind of integrity. This was an anomaly lately,
as I thought of Hope in Arkansas, Raton in New Mexico,
maybe Milford in Delaware.

And maybe the arts did, in fact, fortify a town's resil-
ience to the threat of sprawl and its wave of decay. For
instance, NashArts, my presenting organization here,

----

88 http://media.dissonantstates.com/i/Traffic.jpg

made its home in a once-derelict church. Richard, its new director, greeted me from inside. The first thing I noticed was that the pews were still in place. Then I saw the Baldwin grand piano on the stage.

"It's getting a little tune-up later," Richard said as I walked to the piano. He looked like a young outdoorsmen in his tee shirt, shorts, and hiking sneakers. Scattered throughout the space were paintings, quilts, photographs, and pieces of phallic wooden art.

"So does this still function as a church?" I asked, but Richard was gone.

"Nope," his voice answered from another room. "Well, yes! A church of art! Oh, I forgot to tell you," he appeared again. "Our guests have a special rate at the Hampton Inn about ten minutes down the road. Fifty dollars a night."

So far in America 88x50, my CD and donation revenue had exceeded anything I'd ever anticipated. The numbers weren't in, mainly because I wasn't counting, but the cash stuffed in my car console was keeping me buoyed on the road, and dropping fifty bucks on a nice hotel for once, while not quite in keeping with my project's fading mission statement of roughing it on the road, didn't strike me as especially egregious. Nashville didn't have a campground or hostel, I imagined, and maybe the Hampton Inn had a pool!

So before long I was describing America 88x50 to a receptionist at the Hampton Inn registration desk. "The music sounds *gorgeous!*" she said in her warm, southern accent.

"You'll have to come and see!"

She typed a few final keystrokes with gusto. "Okay, we have it all set up through NashArts! You don't have to worry about anything, Adam. Just sign right there."

"Hm?"

"Is everything all right?" Even as her brow furrowed she maintained her cheer.

"The room was billed to NashArts?" I asked.

"Yes, and your room key is processing right now."

I glimpsed the front page of a complimentary *USA Today* that read IT FINALLY HAPPENS: GAS $3.00! Suddenly the wad of cash in my console seemed much, much smaller, and I didn't feel all so guilty about whatever miscommunication led to my getting a free room that night.

"Where's your next show?" she asked.

I looked up and smiled. "Florida."

She laughed and repeated the word to herself, and then quickly brought herself back. "Did you ever think there was a Nashville, North Carolina?"

"No," I said. "And when I tell people I'm playing here, they argue with me."

"Do they think you mean Tennessee?"

"Actually, they think I mean Asheville."

She handed me a plastic key card. "Well, welcome to *Nashville*, North Carolina! I wish you the best of luck tomorrow! And just so you know, we have a Manager's Assembly down the hall here from seven to nine tonight."

"So stay out?"

"No," she laughed. "Free pizza and beer! Relax."

☆

I spent the next day reading Bach on the Baldwin. At one point, Richard walked by and I stopped. "Just so you know, this isn't what I'm playing tonight," I apologized. "I just play it sometimes to warm up my brain and my bod—"

"I know *nothing* about classical music," he replied. "Sounds good to me!"

I went to the bathroom. What came out of me looked like deer pellets. Nerves? My colitis? I noticed posters on the wall advertising everything except America 88x50. I should have my own poster that I provide to everyone who hosts me, I thought. Why didn't I do that? Then I stared into the mirror at my continually pimpled face—the colitis meds, it had to be—and felt completely sick of myself, sick *with* myself. An hour to go before showtime, I changed my clothes and put on some tinted zit cream, which lately I was using as a kind of makeup.

Tonight Richard said it, and a couple days before him it was Andrew, and so on and so on, these strange post-show confessions from several of my hosts that they would have put more effort into promoting America 88x50 had they "only known." Only known what? That I wasn't just *pretending* to be a pianist touring the country playing piano recitals? Pretending to be a pianist touring the country...I repeated the phrase in my mind a couple times. Well, hadn't this been my fear all along? That I was just pretending to be a concert pianist? When had that stopped? Maybe it was a side effect of playing for so many empty halls and hearing all these *shoulda woulda couldas* from my hosts, but something had indeed shifted, and I began to feel defensive in a way that wasn't rooted in insecurity, which was typical, but rather in confidence, in a sense of deserving, which was new.

"Did they at least give you a good deal at the Hampton Inn?" Richard asked.

"Yes, a great deal!" I said, with the guilt lasting only about as many seconds as I had audience members. Thirteen, maybe?

VERO BEACH, FLORIDA

I zipped down the Florida coastline in my shiny blue car, sunroof open, sunglasses on, shirt off, reggae music blasting, feeling like a king, no longer a solemn missionary of neglected American music but a hit man, here to do my job and get on my way. When people asked what my Vermont license plate was doing all the way in Florida, I answered that I was *on tour*. I might as well have pulled my sunglasses down onto the bridge of my nose with my index finger and added, "Fifty states."

I conveniently omitted that, though the tour's halfway mark was just around the corner, I was about twenty-five states short. But what of it? I had the bright, salty air and warm aqua water to nourish my body and feed my spirit in a way that practicing and cold-calling venues never could.

I arrived at Vero Beach's Academy of Performing Arts, my venue, to find that it was holding its annual open house the day of my recital. The Academy was housed within a church complex, and my concert would take place in a magnificent sanctuary with multiple stages, a giant organ, a high ceiling, and room for hundreds, maybe thousands of worshipers. Everything looked new, unsmeared, and unstained by a public that, over time, would surely wear it down just by showing up. Shiny wood glimmered in the light of immaculate bluish-green windows and carpet. At the entrance, I noticed that someone had placed a hat for donations that would benefit the academy. I looked around for somewhere else to put my CDs and wondered where I could find another hat.

I had a pretty good showing, people of all ages, and in the middle of them I could see my aunt and younger cousin who had driven up to Vero Beach from Boca Raton, the first family members I'd seen in America 88x50 since my other cousin in Chicago.

Heather[89], the administrator with whom I'd set up the concert, stood onstage beside the piano[90] addressing the crowd. "Now, the moment you've all been waiting for!" I felt my chest rise with pride. *Show 'em what you got, Tendler!*

"The raffle results!"

Ah, of course, the raffle results. Heather announced the winner of a new guitar, and there was a mass exodus out of the sanctuary, virtually emptying it but for my two family members and a couple stragglers who looked utterly lost amid the rows of empty pews. Then she introduced me. I began walking toward the instrument from offstage to the dreadful accompaniment of those few people clapping in solidarity—I could hear

89 http://dissonantstates.com/post/11143516199/balladofheather
90 http://media.dissonantstates.com/i/VeroBeachPiano.jpg

each single clap echoing—and then even that stopped. I was still walking, not even halfway there, and I could hear my shoes squeaking on the waxed wooden floor. Dead silence, still walking, thinking to myself, *if a recital tour hits all fifty states but no one's there to hear it, does it make a sound?*

At last, I stopped at the piano bench, turned obediently toward the silence, and bowed.

NASHVILLE, TENNESSEE

I went on two dates, if you could call them that, with Jennifer when we were both students at Indiana. She was a fantastic pianist, attractive—every guy wanted her—and even though I knew I was incapable of really *dating* her, I had some strange idea that I should try. Besides, I knew my public love life was less about romance and more about fulfilling a sense of responsibility, defying those people whispering behind my back. And it was never about sex or love.

Our dates involved coffee and shoptalk, discussions about repertoire, recitals, our respective musical histories, and methods of practicing. She'd over practiced and nearly destroyed her wrist while at IU, which gave us a lot to talk about. I'm sure I paid for the coffee, but I'm also sure we never kissed.

After we both left IU, we remained friends over e-mail. She divorced classical music and went to Nashville to pursue a career in popular music, and also taught at a local music school. I e-mailed her a month into the tour and asked if she could think of a way I could bring

America 88x50 to Nashville for my Tennessee show. "Sure," she'd written back. "We can do it in my studio."

While practicing[91] before the concert, I got a call from my older sister Candace in San Francisco. "Guess who's on her way right now?" It turned out that her childhood best friend, whom I'd essentially grown up with too, now lived in Nashville and would be attending my show with her husband, daughter, and sister Jody. "They just want to know that they will have seats," Candace said.

"They'll be fine," I answered flatly, looking at the empty room.

But in fact, it wasn't long before the studio was filled to capacity with Jennifer's students and their parents, all chomping on popcorn—a nod to Sandpoint—and sipping bottled water that she and her boyfriend had bought. My sister's friend, her sister Jody, and the rest of her family sat in the back, and they all endured the recital patiently, leaving at the end as I received a standing ovation. Everyone except Jody, that is, who stayed and strolled with me outside toward her Corolla. "I want to buy seven CDs," she announced once we reached the car. "And I want to pray for you."

"Sorry?"

She scribbled out a check and placed it halfway in her jeans pocket before putting her hand in mine and holding it tight, raising it into the air and waving it back and forth against the black Nashville sky. Her other hand held onto the Corolla's roof for balance. She closed her eyes. "Dear Lord Jesus, bless Adam as he searches for

91 http://dissonantstates.com/post/5688346725/tennessee#atlanta

his place in this world. Lord, keep him safe as he makes his way through different opportunities and challenges. Bless his state of mind regardless of what he chooses or where he finally lands." Several people I recognized from the audience drove by and I smiled nervously as they passed, struggling to keep my eyes closed. But then, oddly enough, by the time Jody finished my baptism I really *did* feel renewed. The streetlights looked brighter, the scent of vanilla wafting out of Jody's Corolla from the air fresheners hanging on her rearview mirror smelled sweet and exotic. It was a miracle. I wondered how long it would last. She lowered our locked hands, let go, and handed me the check from her pocket. We hugged.

"Thank you," I whispered.

That night, laying on a futon in a loft above her garage, I thought of Jennifer and her boyfriend, how effortless it must be for them to love each other, to make love, to make a life. She could engage him and he her, and they were free to please each other and complete each other like it was nothing. God, I resented them. I felt like my emotional will had been severed at birth from my body's ability to execute it. I wanted to be straight, but my body just wouldn't, *couldn't* let me—that was what I told myself—and it was agonizing to come face to face with such powerlessness, feeling like a passenger to my own being, especially as a pianist. A classical musician's livelihood, after all, is based in large part upon transforming notes on a page, notes which at first may seem impossible, into music that sounds effortless and organic. All it requires is time, work, patience, discipline, and strategy, and this combination eventually becomes something we call talent. Why couldn't I apply such a principle to the rest of my life? Why couldn't I work myself straight? Why couldn't *that* be my talent?

Whether it was self-acceptance, or love, or control that I craved, I was probably looking for all of it in the wrong places out here in the concert halls and highways and chat rooms of America 88x50. And yet I was drawn to see this pursuit, this tour, to its logical end, even if that logical end might be some terrible collapse and a huge disappointment, an end where I would still be a nobody, still in the closet, and still unable to play a concert without forgetting half the notes. But it's as if part of me wanted to someday watch it all fall apart, if for no other reason than to prove to myself that in the end at least I was right about *something*.

DEWEES ISLAND, SOUTH CAROLINA

Naked, I fell to my knees, and a muddy wave hit the front of my body with a crack, pulverizing me backward into the sand. An icy mix of seawater and shells washed over and into every crevice of my body. I breached from the foam against an ominous gray sky and staggered there, digging my heels into the ocean floor, fighting against that furious current, demanding, enticing me even, to let go and just ride endlessly out into oblivion. Another brown wave curled overhead and I pounced forward into it. With a punch, it sent me somersaulting underwater. The top of my left foot collided with the ocean floor and a painful release shot through my body along with the sound, an inward echo, of all my toes shattering. I stood up and, teetering on one leg, lifted my foot above the surface. My toes were crooked and bleeding. I studied my body further, and discovered blood dripping down my arms, my back, around my neck and down my chest.

This violent tide and dirty water[92] would be the extent of South Carolina's brush with Hurricane Katrina, and my mangled foot and flayed skin were mere kisses from a storm whose name I'd yet to even hear, but whose aftermath in the coming months I would know better than I could have ever predicted. Limping a few paces deeper, I growled, "One more."

On a golf cart, the only mode of transportation on Dewees Island, I bounced down a narrow dirt path to Jane's house, a swelling fortress with beautiful shutters and porches jutting out in all directions. The tiny road ended there[93], while all of the other mansions on the island were tucked and hidden behind the thick wall of palms that lined both sides of the tiny road[94], houses accessible only by discreet driveways the size of footpaths that branched off into the bushes. Every property was beachfront. The inside of the house smelled like a seafood restaurant. Jane[95]

92 http://media.dissonantstates.com/i/DeweesCoast.jpg

93 http://media.dissonantstates.com/i/JanesHouse.jpg

94 http://media.dissonantstates.com/i/DeweesRoad.jpg

95 http://dissonantstates.com/post/11411038436/balladofjane

was hosting a dinner party[96] that night with her husband, a man of few words whom I seldom saw. Like a small bird, Jane fluttered about the kitchen with a knife, cutting vegetables. She was frail but full of energy and seemed to have perfected her own style of acerbic wit.

"You actually swam?" she asked, looking up from the cutting board. "Are you suicidal? And did you swing by the meeting house to see the digital piano you've been having nightmares about?" She went back to designing her salad.

I tried to laugh. "Not yet. It'll be fine. I haven't been having nightmares."

"Oh, come on. I get it. You needed a show. We're state twenty-three. You're too close to the halfway mark to turn anything down." A friend of Jane's on the mainland who ran an art center had referred me to her, and this had indeed been my only South Carolina option, and I had indeed resisted until the last minute, and I had indeed been having nightmares about doing this program on a digital piano.

"I think I might have just broken one of my toes," I said, changing the subject. The bleeding had stopped, but my right foot's middle toe had turned purple and clung like a frightened child to the index toe beside it.

Jane walked over and peered down at my foot with the half-interest of a mechanic examining a broken fuel gauge. "Yes, it's broken." She returned to the counter.

I'd never broken anything before. "Is it going to be okay?"

_____

96 http://dissonantstates.com/post/6108318719/southcarolina#party

"You can't do anything, really. But I'll make you a splint." She pulled open a drawer, found a small wooden coffee stirrer, and snapped it in two. "This will be perfect."

I choose a bathroom—there are several—turn the shower on as hot and possible, and sit on a wooden bench inside the glass shower stall as the water streams past me and steams the room. My body's muscles, hardened from the sea, ease into the steam, and I can taste the saltwater melting off my skin and out of my pores. I lean against the wall, and, for the first time in months, release what I've let store up inside me in all those motel rooms, so turned on am I still by my angry, naked, broken-bone tryst with Katrina.

The next day, I rearranged the meetinghouse near the dock where I would perform, creating a flow of couches, lamps, tables, chairs, and, of course, the keyboard[97]. Jane was there for a moment but left before I started practicing. "Don't wear yourself out, and call me when you're finished. When do you think that'll be? An hour?"

"Yeah, sure…" I said, staring into the illuminated interface of the Roland keyboard, puzzled over why every time I pressed the soft pedal all of the notes would automatically tune down a half-step. The nightmare had begun.

Four hours later, I called Jane.

97 http://media.dissonantstates.com/i/DeweesRoland.jpg

I hadn't planned on taking so long, but an electric piano hides nothing, has no sympathy, no mercy. On an acoustic piano, even a bad one, pianists have the cushion of resonance, the psychological security of an instrument working *with* them, on their behalf. But on a digital piano, there's no *real* resonance, no *real* mechanism, even as "weighted" as the keys may be. Every note feels unsupported, vulnerable, and every slip feels extra exposed, extra empty and cold. I was having a lot of slips, as it were, and, in a panic, started jamming my fingers into the keyboard, grinding them into and in between the keys as they cracked and popped, almost as if I intended to smudge out what felt like several days' worth of tension and non-practice. It seemed like my arms were glued to the sides of my body, and I swung and stretched them behind my back and across the front of my body to loosen up. I felt claustrophobic. Was I sweating? My legs hovered over the floor, not at all grounded, swaying and curling beneath the piano bench. And through it all, my mind was screaming that *this is all because you jerked off yesterday!*

I heard Jane's golf cart crunching over the gravel. "We have…no time!" she called from the parking lot as I ran to her. "The concert's in less than an hour!" She accelerated before I even sat down, and I grabbed one of the cart's side railings to keep from flying off. Jane zoomed down the path toward home, hitting potholes that bounced us into the air, driving onto banks to avoid puddles, nearly somersaulting the vehicle. When other drivers approached, she swerved away from them at the last second, as if playing chicken. She was crazed, panicked, speaking little, and when she did, it was stream-of-conscious. "I made biscuits! We'll get dressed at home! I need to walk the dog!"

All the while, a black cloud overhead looked like it was about ready to swallow Dewees Island. "Look at that!" I said in disbelief as we drove toward it.

"I'm making a conscious decision *not* to look at that!" she answered.

By the time we arrived at home it was pouring. Jane bolted from the cart before it came to a stop and ran inside. I put some peanut butter on one of her biscuits as she rounded up the dog. I stuffed my CDs and Jane's shoes into a plastic supermarket bag—she liked to drive barefoot—and volunteered to hold the food we needed to bring, grabbing a tray covered with aluminum foil. She walked the dog in three minutes and was back with me at the door.

With a motherly tenderness, she began tugging at the collar of the raincoat she'd just leant me. "And you're really okay with this?"

"It's perfect," I said. "Thank you." Through over-heard snippets of conversation, I'd picked up that she had recently lost her son, but I didn't know when, and I didn't ask how.

"Okay," she said, abandoning my collar. "Ready? Here we go!" She kicked open the door and we launched into the storm. The show was supposed to start in ten minutes.

"We'll probably be the last ones there!" I shouted through the deafening rain, falling around us like bullets. "Or late! Just tell them I had a nervous breakdown!"

"They'd love that!" she shrieked, turning the wheel wildly to avoid a flood in the road. "I think we're all waiting for you to have a nervous breakdown."

☆

Candles burn as warm tropical wind blows in through the screens. Heavy rain showers pummel the roof of the cottage house. The place is packed. Jane sits in the back, still wearing her raincoat. Does the music sound like it would on an acoustic piano? No. But does it work? Here, right now? Yes. As its faithful ambassador, I'm sweating through my clothes trying to help it across the digital Rubicon, not unlike my performance on the dilapidated upright in Bigfork, and there's a moment within each piece when I have to let go. I'm faced with the decision to either resist or accept the challenges of this piano and my limits as a pianist to surmount them—*I cannot make this Roland sound like a Fazioli*—and so I choose to enjoy. Enjoy the heat of the candles, the sound of the rain, the steamy breeze, the encouragement of these strangers who almost definitely have never in their lives heard a note of this music until tonight. All of us together in this meeting room with the last ferry long gone and a hurricane whipping the ocean around us into a rage. All of us happy to be here.

MARION, VIRGINIA

My money disappeared into a cash register festooned with a series of photocopied pictures taped left to right of Hitler, then Mussolini, and then Bill Clinton. I left and returned to the interstate, rejoining tens of thousands of racing enthusiasts who were making their pilgrimage to Bristol, home of NASCAR. I myself was inching along with them, but not toward Bristol, but to Marion, home of the Lincoln Theatre, and a town unfortunate enough to be on the way. In fact, I needed to get to the theater as soon as possible to pick up keys to a stranger's trailer. She was going to the races and had volunteered her place for the night. It was amazing how people just trusted a concert pianist.

Finally in Marion, I pulled in front of the Lincoln Theatre. Its marquee read PIANIST ADAM TENDLER[98] and I stepped out of my car to snap a photo, feeling the town's eyes on me, even though there was no one in sight.

Daveena, the theater's director, met me in the Lincoln lobby and handed me the keys and directions to the volunteer's trailer. "I think she's waiting for you there, but before you go, would you like to have a look around the inside of the theater?"

"Sure!" I said. The lobby floor inclined slightly, with wall-length windows on one side revealing a neighboring department clothing store. "Is this typical for buildings in this region?" I asked. "Indoor windows that look into other buildings?"

It was as if Daveena had never noticed that you could watch people shop for underwear from the Lincoln Theatre lobby. "I don't know," she said. Maybe it was a silly question.

After unlocking two doors that I thought would lead straight into the hall, she led me down another corridor, this one adorned with what looked like Latin American art and sculptures. "The Lincoln is one of the country's only remaining Mayan theaters," she said, weaving an invisible ribbon with her hand toward the décor as we walked. I had no idea what she was talking about—a Mayan theater? in the US?—but her

---

98 http://media.dissonantstates.com/i/MarionMarquee.jpg

Southern voice comforted me, and I nodded my head in delight. At last, the hallway emptied into an auditorium, and yes, the architecture looked, well, pretty Mayan, even if the walls were covered with enormous panels[99] depicting colonial scenes. "Aren't they beautiful?" Daveena said, looking up. "They were painted by high school students a long time ago. We just barely had them restored. Before that, they had all kinds of cobwebs and bird poop on them."

The piano[100] was shoved into a corner below the stage. I remembered just then that in this concert I would perform off of the stage, down on the floor at seat level. This, for all intents, was probably a rehearsal piano. I walked over and lifted the cover. Chickering.

"Do you recognize that brand? Is it good?" she asked.

"I know the name," I answered, "which is better than *not* knowing the name." I played some chords and a few quiet passages from my program. The piano sounded slightly out of tune and had very heavy keys, but as custom, I turned to my host with a grin. "Great!"

"Good. We just had it tuned last week. You're not allergic to cats, are you?"

"No," I lied.

"Do you like them?"

"Yes," I lied again.

"Good, because the woman who's letting you stay at her trailer has this Siamese cat, a really hateful creature. I'd stay out of its way if I were you."

99 http://media.dissonantstates.com/i/MarionPanels1.jpg

100 http://media.dissonantstates.com/i/MarionPiano.jpg

The owner of the trailer was a short woman with buzzed gray hair. She showed me around the small quarters and gave some pointed advice about how to keep the front door open at all times so Russell, the cat, could come and go as he pleased. There he was in the bedroom doorway, staring out at us. "Russell thinks everything is his," she warned. "It's fine so long as you keep your distance." She looked over at Russell with an encouraging, sympathetic frown, and then went over to pet him, a gesture he accepted for a few seconds before swatting wickedly at her hand. She withdrew fast and looked at me smiling. "See?"

My mouth began to form something, though I couldn't quite predict what it planned to say. The word was: "Why?"

"He ain't adopted or anything. Just always been this way. I've had him since a baby. He's just a bad cat." She stood up and left Russell by the bed. "So, make yourself at home. You can use that computer there." She motioned to an old IBM with a frenzied Halloween-themed screensaver drawing gravestones across the display and scrawling RIP on each tomb. "Just try not to let that screen bother you. My niece put it up there last Halloween and I can't get it off. If you know how to fix it, by all means…"

I just laughed. "It doesn't bother me, but if you want me to—"

"And this is the TV, in case you want to watch the races tonight."

"Maybe."

"I'm not really even going to the races. I'm just going to a *party* where they're watching them. The whole thing's just an excuse to drink. Some mornings after the races I wake up and can't believe my car's even parked outside—never mind the fact that it's on top of the mailbox!"

And with a laugh, she was out the door, leaving me alone with Russell. Just when her car disappeared, he emerged from the bedroom, strolling toward me and rubbing against my leg. Then he backed away and sat down facing me, as if extending an invitation to approach. Or a dare. With the image of him swatting his owner still fresh in my memory, I kept away. Besides, I was hungry. I grabbed my keys and walked out the door, leaving the TV on for Russell.

In the café across the street from The Lincoln, the guy who made my turkey wrap had scruffy hair, a goatee, and glasses. He'd just left the army and, upon his return to Marion, had let his hair grow and his body to fall out of shape. When I asked, he said he'd never go back to the military, and when I asked why, said he'd rather not talk about it. The girl who rang me up looked about nineteen. Her fiancé had also just returned from Iraq.

While I ate, the conversation turned somehow to horror movies, how they liked them, how my father used to watch them with me during our weekends together, how those movies inspired my early creative life[101], and how Marion had its own array of haunted spots. I heard ghost story after ghost story, personal accounts and tales my new friends had heard from others.

---

101 http://dissonantstates.com/post/1003818512/fatallipstick

It was new for me to engage people out in the world like this, and for a rare moment, I felt like the warm, jovial guy I'd always hoped I could be—magnetic and interesting and personable, having adventures and meeting new people instead of staying holed up in motel rooms as the nation I set out to explore swirled about outside.

"Let's all go on a ghost hunt tonight!" I cried, and the second the words came out I wished to take them back. "You can bring your fiancé!" I continued, to my own disbelief. "Didn't you say he loves horror movies?" It was like I had no control over my words, as if I was possessed. "Or we could all watch movies at the trailer where I'm staying! I've got the place to myself." My face went flush and I bit my lip, almost to keep my mouth from opening again. Was I really this lonely? This desperate? I'd had no idea.

"My fiancé likes scary movies," said the girl, "but he won't go back to any of those places we told you about. He already has enough nightmares because of the war and all." Her scruffy co-worker, the veteran, paused his activity of replenishing the condiments, and looked in her direction for a second. Wordlessly, they both resumed cleaning.

Never again, I told myself. Never pull a stunt like that again. Just then, the cashier's fiancé swung through the front door wearing ATV riding gear and a dark green racing hat with a ragged, curved bill. As if it was my cue, I stood up, said goodnight, and walked out the door as he called from behind, saying it was nice to meet me and that I was certainly welcome to stay and hang.

☆

I kept that fiancé's greasy image fresh in my memory when I returned to the trailer, scouring the Internet for someone just like him, someone tortured, someone who couldn't sleep at night, someone who had a secret and who might be willing to create a new one with me. Tonight. All the while, spooked by those ghost stories, I kept expecting a poltergeist to poke its head in the window or appear at Russell's always-open front door. I turned the races on the TV and blasted them at full volume, but was immersed in the distraction of my task with increasing fervency, chatting with whomever I could—*I'm in Marion, U? I'm in Marion, U? I'm in Marion, U?*—but nothing was happening, no one was out there, and hours later I was curled up in bed listening to the cars and tractor-trailers passing on the dark strip of highway below the trailer, ashamed that I'd wasted my night on the computer and come up empty-handed when I could have been sleeping. Tomorrow's concert[102] would start at two p.m., my earliest show yet, now less than twelve hours away.

Russell nestled his warm body between my calves—he wasn't such a bad cat—and I thought of high school, the Army, and a boy named Calvin[103]. I was a sophomore in high school, and he went to Norwich University. We met during a winter survival course in the woods, something I participated in with my high school outing club, which itself was an extra-curricular group that I was only participating in (and treasurer of) to impress the teacher who ran it[104], as I would've done anything to

---

102 http://dissonantstates.com/post/11534062932/virginiafragment
103 http://dissonantstates.com/post/7108400430/seventakesofcalvin
104 http://dissonantstates.com/post/11732826815/balladoftodd

impress him. Case in point. There I was in mid-February, fingers freezing, surrounded by young men in uniform, learning how to make animal traps, build snow forts, start fires in the woods, and kill and skin chickens without using a knife.

"What's your name?" whispered a tan boy next to me during the latter lesson.

"Adam."

"Calvin."

That night, we all piled into a circular army tent with a wood stove in the corner. Everyone, both male and female, was pressed up against the other, and Calvin put his sleeping bag next to mine. He was captivated by the fact that my oldest sister who lived in Malibu had once been in *Playboy*, and that I was a classical pianist who planned to go music school. I liked that he was Hawaiian and had once worked in the rodeo as a cowboy. Surrounding us, the boisterous group of cadets traded stories of their military trips abroad. I listened, admiring them. They were only slightly older than me, and yet they had been everywhere, it seemed. I wanted to travel, too. Then I felt a frigid hand on my bare stomach. "My hands are cold," whispered Calvin.

"Okay," I said. We had, after all, learned this technique earlier—how to warm your hands with a friend. Then he began rubbing. That wasn't in the lesson. I froze with fear. This had to be a trap. Any minute now he would throw over the sleeping bag and expose me to the group. I would hear that word. They would call me a faggot. The icy hand traced down my stomach and found the fold of my underwear, and Calvin's finger slipped between the elastic waistband and my skin.

"You don't want to do that," I warned.

"I do."

Laughter erupted across the tent. I tensed, adrenaline shooting through my abdomen and legs. This was it, the moment when everyone would know, but it was just the cadets laughing at someone's joke, and Calvin heard it too, shouting his own two cents into the crossfire, his unseen hand still tucked into my underwear. And, laughing with the group, he reached further and grabbed. I was breathless, in a cold sweat, and exhilarated by the idea that this person *knew* I wanted him, was holding the proof in his hand, and yet didn't find it, or me, or the situation, repulsive. "I'll wake you once everyone's asleep and it's my turn to watch the fire," he whispered.

A few hours later, he did. There, in an army tent in the dead of winter, surrounded by more than a dozen sleeping cadets, and just a few days before my seventeenth birthday, Calvin was my first kiss.

PART TWO

WELLFLEET,
MASSACHUSETTS

I grew up in Barre, Vermont, the blue-collar center of the most liberal state in the union, its name once determined by a fistfight. It's a place for posturing. Men strut with chests out and bodies bobbing from side to side. I could do it, too, if I tried, but I didn't do much strutting about Main Street once I returned home for my sister Candace's wedding. I stayed in my mom's and stepfather's log cabin on the outskirts of town, holed up in the piano studio above the garage practicing for my one September concert—Massachusetts, on Cape Cod—and calling prospective hosts. Having twenty-four states behind me made no real difference to anyone, it seemed, and my proposals were met with as much dismissal and suspicion as ever. I found a sensible web designer who worked out of an old farmhouse nearby, and we created the America

88x50 website[105], complete with reviews and sound files, to which I started directing the people I called. Still nothing. Truly, there was no formula in offering people free piano recitals of modern American music.

Meanwhile, Candace called every day from San Francisco to double-check on wedding details with my mother. And I was sneaking away to chat on my cell phone with a guy named Shane who lived in Spokane, a guy I met in a chat room online, a guy who in a week's time I was talking to several times a day, a guy who a week later booked an airline ticket to meet me during my upcoming October residency in Reno. He would fly in from Spokane and we'd split the cost of a week's stay at the Atlantis Casino Resort Motor Lodge. As the plan went, during the day I would visit local schools with my host, performing and discussing the music of 88x50 with Reno elementary school students, and at night I would come back to Shane. With the single purchase of a plane ticket, Shane was instantly and inseparably woven into the tapestry of America 88x50.

Till then, we had the cell phone, and each night we drifted to sleep together while talking on it. I had never felt anything like this, so wanted, and just hearing his soft and scratchy voice would send me squirming into myself, queasy and happy and warm, with something new blossoming in the pit of my stomach where there were usually just nerves. On the phone, he'd talk about his life and I'd stretch out and smile like a lounging cat.

Shane's job at the time was to travel around and refill stuffed animals into those arcade games like the one I saw at Denny's in Raton. I told him how I hated those

---

105 http://www.america88x50.com

things, how I'd never seen anyone win any prizes, and he only laughed. "Some people win, buddy. It just depends on how tightened the claw is." That was the night before my concert at Wellfleet Public Library. I stayed alone in a cabin by the ocean, an accommodation arranged by the library, and Shane sang me to sleep with a country ballad.

No standing ovation could compare to how he made me feel, a feeling of being adored for simply...I don't know...for answering the phone. For existing. I felt safe with his voice, like I had nothing to hide. And I didn't. We already knew each other's big secret from day one, and with that out of the way, we could grow, and we were growing fast, tumbling into *I love you*s over the phone like children, not knowing or caring what it meant to say these things to someone we'd never really met.

So was this me submitting, once and for all, to all those voices in my head, all the voices of everyone in the past, that chorus of accusations? Was I finally answering yes? Sure, no one knew about Shane, and our Reno rendezvous would happen behind a closed motel room door, but I guess it didn't matter. It was becoming painfully obvious as I gave into these feelings for him that the conventional boy-girl model for love and marriage I grew up wanting so badly, a rite I would witness and participate in for my sister in just a few days, and which I still probably *wished* I could pull off myself, was a fantasy, at least for me, and playing into that model, once so routine and automatic, now felt like a hopelessly indefinite charade, a masquerade that everyone seemed to be just waiting for me to end—a matter of when, not if. In the meantime, freedom for me was on the other end of that cell phone with Shane, or in those rare, perfect moments at the piano when everything fit and I was out of my own way. Pure being. My concerts had for some time served as my own public confessions of the nameless, where everywhere else in my life I seemed to function from behind a façade, a performance of another kind, an act I'd cultivated since pre-school and refined the more I grew and observed, like any performer, what worked and what didn't.

With Calvin as an exception, until now I'd prided myself on my discipline of repression, give or take those couple of lapses, those sporadic rolls in the hay with a guy here or there, from which I'd typically rally sick with guilt but brimming with rationalizations. That urge, so I'd once told myself, only gained power with resistance, like a sneeze you try to suppress until it explodes all over the place, and as long as I *knew* the straight and narrow and *wanted* the straight and narrow, then I'd be fine; a lapse was just a lapse, and these things happen.

That was then. Now there were several versions of me arguing back and forth, competing for attention. One was giving in to Shane, another still wished to be straight, and another was stuck in the middle, unable to tell left from right, up from down, but only knew what felt right in that moment and what also didn't feel good *anymore.* Illuminating as this might seem, it didn't *feel* liberating at the time, this coming into my own, this dissonance between my different selves. It felt more like being attached to a diseased and dying Siamese twin, watching it decay but having no idea how to detach. I wasn't that strong, so I thought, not that courageous. Coming out was something I'd always thought about, but never thought I could really go through with, like suicide.

CLEVELAND, OHIO

During my month in Vermont, my mom and I would occasionally bring food and supplies to Montpelier where volunteer groups collected donations for the people who, at that very moment, were stranded and dying in the aftermath of Katrina. Not that I had any concerts lined up in the South—not Louisiana, not Alabama, not Mississippi, not Texas—but Hurricane Katrina had already affected my tour. It went beyond the fact that gas was now over three dollars a gallon. The country was in shock and very much in mourning; nothing could be trusted, and everything was a threat—the sky, the sea, the government—and here I was, still calling people I didn't know and proposing my little piano recitals. It suddenly seemed kind of weird—what was I doing?— and yet at the same time I wondered if the music of 88x50 might now provide solace to its listeners, presenting an American musical portrait the likes of which they could actually value for its honesty, now that our collective idealism was shot, discontent widespread, and our imperfect country so devastatingly exposed in the wake of Katrina. Before September, my choice in music might have taken some audiences by surprise—maybe its dissonance seemed somehow un-American—but now I wondered if, instead of pining for basic Americana, people might better recognize and appreciate the complexity, the necessary bite of this music, and, therefore, come to savor its unique beauty. I guess I'd find out. I just had to remember to notice.

Driving to Ohio, I listened on public radio to the sobs of survivors, statistics of unimaginable destruction, tales of people starving, senior citizens found dead in nursing homes, families trapped in their attics, inmates drowning in their jail cells.

After having already driven across the United States twice in three months, I internalized more than anything else that it took only a little patience and a bit of gas to get anywhere in this country, which made all that untold suffering in the South, at least for me, seem unbearably close. *My God*, I remember thinking. *I could drive there from here. And I will.*

It was raining in Cleveland. Police cars and an ambulance swarmed a Kentucky Fried Chicken near the Broadway School of Music[106]. There was one man in handcuffs, a woman shaking with her hands over her mouth, and another man, overweight, shirtless, and in a stretcher, with tubes coming out of his face. Barbara, who directed the school, told me to expect a "diverse and industrial"[107] community when we confirmed the concert just a week or so earlier on the phone.

Now she and I were folding programs as a small audience filed into its little recital hall. I hadn't performed this music for several weeks now and hadn't touched a piano in days before that afternoon, practicing in the hall[108], so when I finally began playing before this audience, it was like my ears had a new distance, a new sense of discovery, as if part of me was sharing

---

106 http://media.dissonantstates.com/i/BroadwaySchool.jpg

107 http://dissonantstates.com/post/11651797748/ohiofragment

108 http://media.dissonantstates.com/i/BroadwayRecitalHall.jpg

in the listening with them. Of course, sometimes this went too far and I *really* didn't know what the fuck was coming next, so in the intermission, I rushed to a side room and began rummaging through my scores, checking passages where I'd slipped and reviewing the spots coming up where I doubted my memory. And when I came out of the room, I ran into a short, bearded man whom I'd noticed limply clapping between the pieces. "So what do you think?" I asked, and he seemed relieved by the question.

"How much of your program was influenced by World War II?" he asked.

"Maybe a lot of it," I said, though I didn't really know. Little was known about the emotional origins of this music because the composers had revealed so little. Still, the more the man and I talked, the more I realized that his impression of the music was what really mattered, anyway, and what I mistook all along for his aloofness was in fact a deep sense of contemplation. "There are *bombs*[109] in the Ginastera," he said. "I hear explosions and screams everywhere. He composed the piece in 1944?" I nodded, and he seemed to think a moment. "I'll tell you what makes this music American: the screams."

DENVER, COLORADO

Eighty-eight. Eighty-eight in a seventy-five—my third speeding ticket—and again I've been caught in one of my more conservative moments, considering that I burned through the bulk of Kansas going well over a

---

109 http://media.dissonantstates.com/a/GinasteraCrashCrash.mp3

hundred. The officer wishes me well and I squeal back onto Interstate 70 before he makes it back to his squad car. The grind of pavement against tires, the hypnotic dotted white line, the sound of a revving engine, the isolation, the mindless passing of hours, the trance, the speed, the closeness of death, of collision, and the anticipation of the proverbial concert—it all brings me peace. I'm chasing the sun into the west, feeling small and insignificant but on my way. A billboard tells me that ABORTION KILLS WHAT GOD MADE, and just beyond it, another says XXX NOVELTY SUPERSTORE ADULT TOYS VIDEO ARCADE DVD. I'm back in the Bible Belt.

Thanks to the twelve-year-old girl on vacation with her parents in Idaho who introduced herself after my Sandpoint concert and offered to get me a concert at her school in Colorado, I had a show in the main hall[110] of the Denver School of the Arts. "It's so cool that you're, like, still learning," a freckled blonde student said to me after I led a workshop for her piano class. The girl I met in Idaho proudly watched all of this from her seat. "You're still sort of like a student."

"Every night I learn something new about the music and myself," I answered, less than sure that this was entirely true. Sure, my articulation of certain passages had improved, but shouldn't I have had it *all* figured out by now? Shouldn't memory slips and sloppy half-saves of near-disasters have been a thing of the past at

---

110 http://media.dissonantstates.com/i/DenverSchool.jpg

this point in the tour? The whole thing was unclear to me, to what extent I was truly inept at the piano, and how much of it was in my head.

My audience that night stood to their feet in applause. So what did that mean? I made a little over two hundred dollars in CD sales—more than twenty CDs sold. So what did that mean? The chair of the school's piano department wrote on the school's website after my departure: "I think that everyone agrees with me that this recital was an outstanding musical experience. It's wonderful programs like this that show our students what can really be done with the music of the piano." Couldn't I just accept that the tour was working, and that at the end of the day, I was actually pretty good?

Candace's wedding is happening all over again, only this time it's happening during winter. I'm standing on our property at dusk, watching a stream that flows through the woods, raging now because the snow is melting. Or at least it's a version of the stream raging through a version of our woods. Then I notice a snow-mobile zooming through the trees. *He really shouldn't do that,* I think. *Not so late in the season.* And just then the snowmobile topples down a bank and lands upside-down in the stream, instantly submerging its rider in the foaming brown water. I slide and scramble down the bank and plunge in to rescue him, reaching beneath the floating snowmobile for the driver until I finally grab hold of his jacket and pull him to shore. I know he's dead, but pull his helmet off anyway to check. His face is blue, bruised, dented in, and I don't recognize him. I drag him to the house and hide him under the twin bed I grew up sleeping in. I call the police, and as I wait for them to arrive I start to worry that my family will find him first. Just then, the fire trucks, the ambulances, the police cars I summoned begin to approach the house in a blaze of lights and sirens. Everyone will know. My family will ask why I put him under the bed, but I have no idea. None at all. And I wish I'd left him in the stream.

PARK CITY, UTAH

Debra and Fred ran a music school in a two-story strip mall close to the exit for Park City. This was my venue, and the most I would see of Park City during my Utah stay. Downstairs was a pizza parlor, next door, a bar, and across the way, an optometrist's office. The school itself had a number of practice studios and a small concert hall with a brilliantly shined baby grand piano[111]. It also had a small music store, in front of which I set up a table to put two stacks of my CDs on. Fred spoke up from inside the shop, leaning over the glass countertop display by his cash register, his white hair and beard gleaming. "What do you sell those for?"

"To sustain the tour," I said. "It's the only way I can keep it going."

"No, no," he said, shaking his head. "How *much* do you sell them for?"

---

111 http://media.dissonantstates.com/i/ParkCityPiano.jpg

"Only ten dollars. I'll put a little card out here."

He looked concerned. "You know that if we sell them through the store, we'll have to include sales tax, and then take a cut for the store."

My initial thought was to say that it didn't matter since I had no intention whatsoever of selling the CDs through the store, but I had to think carefully in this moment about how to word my response. No presenter had ever as much as implied that they expected a cut of my CDs. After all, these were *donated* recitals, and I never took a cut, even if my hosts charged admission. All I had was my CD sales. "Do we have to sell all of them through the store?"

"People use credit cards around here for everything," he said, his glare unwavering.

For a few seconds, I didn't make a sound. "Sorry, it's just that I've never had this come up before, so I have to think," I muttered. He was still staring straight at me, waiting. "You see, usually people buy the CD as a direct donation to the project, and if they don't have cash, they write a check. And if they don't have a check on them, they take a CD and send a check later to a PO Box I set up in Vermont, which is on my website. I'm usually not manning the CD table to take money, so they either just drop their donation in a basket or give it to a volunteer watching the table. If you want, you could set up your own, separate donation box for the school. Some of my presenters have done that."

"Yeah, but you don't understand," he bristled. "People come in here and use their credit card to buy four-dollar guitar strings!"

"Okay, so are we describing a scenario that involves someone who doesn't use checks, never carries cash, only uses credit cards, and wants a CD?"

"If you sell them for ten, then we'll take five," he said bluntly.

I nearly fell over. He was insane. I'd made these CDs myself, paying for the production, the printing, the packaging, and now, after some quick calculations, I realized Fred's plan had him taking away more profit than me.

"Um," I laughed. "I'm going to put out the jar and people can buy a CD with cash or check. If someone has neither *and* they don't want to send away for it through my website, then they can do it through the store and you can get a cut. That's what we're gonna do." I had the advantage of addressing my audience during the show, and by the time I was done with them, they wouldn't even remember that credit cards existed.

"Okay," he sulked, and didn't speak to me for the rest of the day.

Fred, Debra, their son Aaron[112], a few faculty members, and an elderly couple make up my audience. My playing today has a sloppy uninhibitedness that stems probably from my shame over how few people America 88x50 has attracted, and from guilt over forcing my hosts, whom I've spent all day with, to sit through this concert which they probably have no real interest in anyway. They're attending out of responsibility, I tell myself—kindness, sympathy, obligation. I want to end this whole charade as soon as possible, so I careen through the program like a mad truck driver. Debra records everything

---

112 http://dissonantstates.com/post/11799534005/balladofaaron

live to a CD, and I wonder if its microphone can pick up the cover band next door, playing their Saturday night set. After two hours, the concert ends with the solemn Copland *Sonata*[113] and my hostage audience claps. I bow. They don't stop clapping. Debra's blonde hair bounces and her smile widens. They're still clapping. She turns around to Fred, who sits sternly by himself in the back row, no doubt still pouting about not making a profit off my CD money, a grand total of one ten-dollar bill.

RENO, NEVADA

Highway 50: "The Loneliest Road in America." At least that's what the sign[114] said. Interstate 80 would have taken me straight from Salt Lake City to Reno, which would have been fine, simple enough, but I wanted The Loneliest Road, and so I hooked south onto Highway 93 at the Nevada border, and then west on Highway 50. I always liked looking at the blank spots of an atlas, conjuring up images of what must be there. This appeared to be the most desolate route I could take, and I wanted to see it for myself, the emptiness, the sand dunes[115], the tiny towns, the mountain ranges that looked like crumpled brown paper bags, the straightaway road[116] that has no end. I knew no speed limit. The Loneliest Road was my runway, and I wished to take flight into that bleeding, fiery desert and shoot straight into Reno for the

---

113 http://media.dissonantstates.com/a/PianoSonataUtah.mp3
114 http://media.dissonantstates.com/i/LoneliestRoad.jpg
115 http://media.dissonantstates.com/i/SandDune.jpg
116 http://media.dissonantstates.com/i/Highway50.jpg

riskiest and longest blind date in American piano recital tour-project history.

Shane looked taller in person. I only knew him from pictures, like a celebrity. But there he was, outside the airport terminal, red hair escaping out the sides of a baseball cap, a round face, squinting blue eyes, a goatee; I could even make out the freckles on his fuzzy knuckles. He was wearing a dark green sweater, jeans, and running sneakers. I took him all in at once. This was the moment I had been counting down to for weeks. I had been nervous, but not a dreadful nervousness, more excited, like what anticipating a concert felt like on my best day. I just couldn't wait to align his voice and photographs and e-mails with his actual person. "Look at you!" I said as he crawled into my car, putting my knuckles against his faded orange cap and giving him a noogie. "I can't believe you're here!"

He nudged his elbow across the console into my chest. "Me too, buddy." He always called me buddy.

The Atlantis Resort was a strobe-light hysteria of slot machines, cigarette-smoky carpets, fountains and waterfalls, and hungry gamblers, but we were physically disconnected from it all, to some extent, safe in our Motor Lodge, room 205. "Definitely smells like a motor lodge," Shane said as we entered. I plopped onto the bed and he fell beside me. If he put his hand to my ribcage, he would have felt my heart pulsing just below the surface, fighting against the skin, punching from the inside to get out, to burst into the room and cover everything with its indiscernible contents and save us the trouble of saying the right thing, doing the right thing, thinking the right thing. I wanted my heart to be everywhere.

I felt his breath on my neck, and then the bristle of his face on my lips, against my cheek, and our lips touched, soft and perfect and waiting, but not kissing. We both pulled away and looked into each other. He smirked. He could tell I was scared. I'd done this before, but not with someone I wanted like I wanted him. It had never been like this.

"That wasn't a kiss," he said. "This is a kiss…"

There are only a few hours until I meet Chad, my concert organizer, for another day of outreach perform-ances, when like a pair of musical deliverymen we'll bring modern music to the dilapidated console pianos of Reno's public school cafeterias, sharing excerpts of my program with students and teachers whether they like it or not[117].

But I can't sleep. My thoughts are untraceable and expanding, like two mirrors facing each other on both sides of Shane's and my bed, capturing us for all our endless potential, all our endless inscrutability, extend-ing forever, but not real, just a representation, a reflec-tion behind which there is actually nothing at all, just two guys naked in a bed. And is that so bad? Can't it be that simple? Won't I still be the same pianist, the same artist, still worthy, even if I'm part of that picture?

---

117 http://media.dissonantstates.com/i/RenoDisinterested.jpg

Stop, I tell myself. I don't need to always search for a reason to destroy everything, especially this, to call it bad. I do the same thing onstage during my best moments, when every note falls into place and I feel the need to ruin it, asking myself what note comes next, and then of course everything falls apart, derailing the piece and achieving nothing but the confirmation of the idea that I'm horrible.

He wakes up. "What are you thinking? Why are you awake?"

"Just thinking."

"About me?"

Maybe, if I'm silent, he'll condense and understand everything that's conflicting and consuming my brain without me having to say it, because I know I'll say it wrong if I try. Nothing has cooled in terms of how I feel about him. The love I think I felt in Cape Cod over the phone is still the same love I think I feel right here in room 205, but how can I really love anyone, or anything, if it only reminds me of the part of myself I hate the most? These two states are incompatible, irresolvable, and I feel myself buckling under the weight of their awful dissonance.

"What do you think when you think of me?" he persists.

"That you're inseparable from this whole thing," I say.

"From your life," he concludes.

"Yeah." I pause. "Well, and also from my tour."

☆

This particular school cafeteria had a stage and a small upright, and I stood on the side watching the music teacher introduce me to over a hundred students sitting on the floor below. "Mr. Adam is a professional pianist! He's traveling *all* over the country, visiting *every state!* How many states are there?"

FIFTY!!!

"And now he has come *here* today to play for *you!*"

A small Mexican girl sitting near the front row leaned toward her friend and whispered with her eyes on me and her finger pointing, "Is that the professional?"

Shane stands in the back, his duffel bag at his feet, ready to go to the airport. I play with my back to the room[118], and then welcome a group of hearing-impaired kids to come "feel" the music[119], pressing themselves to the piano. Afterward, he and I hug like friends, and share an unceremonious goodbye. After all, *we* have an audience, too. Or at least, so we think. Then he's gone. Maybe I'll see him in Seattle in a month. Maybe not.

My actual Reno concert a few hours later, at the gallery where Chad works, is a nightmare. I'm sick from a week of school visits and a week of sleepless nights, and my nose drips onto the keyboard as I play. "You look tired," Chad says when I finally stagger from the piano, immediately gulping a vitamin C effervescent solution I prepared beforehand. "You must have had fun with your friend!"

---

118 http://media.dissonantstates.com/i/RenoOutreach.jpg
119 http://media.dissonantstates.com/i/RenoFeelingMusic.jpg

SAN FRANCISCO, CALIFORNIA

On a foldout couch near Fisherman's Warf, I watched the spotlight from Alcatraz Island hit the far wall and slide across the dining room, then the entertainment center, and then back out into San Francisco. I felt contained and unified with it, coming as it did from so far away, and yet landing right here on the wall, just feet away from my pillow, like Tinker Bell flying across the room.

I wanted him beside me, to hear his light snore, to smile in my sleep holding his hand against my heart like I had for that entire week in Reno. I wanted to fit together with someone again like a puzzle piece, to enter him, stay in him, finish in him, claim him as mine. So why in this moment couldn't I even remember his face? It was like in a dream, trying to make out a clock or a calculator or a musical score but never quite getting a clear enough look. Shane's face was shifting in my mind, combining with others, becoming a cartoon, and our time together was taking on mythic proportions, like it, too, was a dream, like it was too magical to have actually happened. Was he a real person who looked out over Reno with me from a viewpoint near Virginia City[120], or was that just a photograph I took? Something inside was slowly devouring Shane's image, our slideshow past, and our fantasy future. Nothing can breathe in a closet, including love, I guess.

The light of Alcatraz breezed by again, and in this moment, I felt alone and contained, but somehow safe within this city and the world beyond it, a world that

120 http://dissonantstates.com/post/11896311603/virginiacity

seemed too large for me to feel any obligation toward it. I owed it nothing, least of which an explanation.

Candace, now a newlywed, navigated me around San Francisco as we made our way to the venue where I would play that night, a piano dealer near downtown. I insisted on opening the sunroof. The air smelled crisp and different to me on the West Coast, cool like the sea, like there was an assuredness, an optimism in the breeze, as if we were all pioneers discovering the Pacific for the first time.

There are only a handful of Fazioli dealers in the world, and only a few Fazioli pianos produced every year. The one I'd perform on tonight, elevated on a small stage at the far end of the gallery, cost just short of two hundred thousand dollars. "I set up around forty or so chairs," said Jim, the piano gallery manager, "just so the place doesn't look empty if I set up more than that and then only forty people come." *Only* forty people? If Jim only knew. He gestured toward the Fazioli onstage. "You ever play on anything like that yet?"

"Yeah," I said. "Actually I have." I studied one summer in Paris and visited the Fazioli dealer in that city. "But not in this tour."

"Well, feel free to go up there and try it out." Jim went back to his desk.

It was nine feet long. The shining gold plate above the soundboard extended and heaved, and the strings were shining like thick threads of gold. The marbleized wood of the piano's inner walls looked like the inside of a Lamborghini. It was so big, this piano, that when I sat at the bench I had to study the keyboard to make sure there weren't more than eighty-eight keys. After all, instead of three pedals, there were four to choose from, including an *extra* soft pedal. From the first notes I played, like perfect drops of melted pearls rising from my fingers up into the room without gravity or limit, I knew that this instrument would take care of me, keep me protected under its strong black wing. At the same time, I felt a heightened sense of responsibility, because if things went badly, I'd have only myself to blame. I couldn't say that the action was giving me trouble *here*, or the balance was out of whack *there*. No, a Fazioli is perfect. It hands the pianist the reigns and wishes them good luck. "I'm a little out of practice," I said to Jim from the bench. "But I'll be in shape by tonight."

"I don't care how you play!" he called back, still staring at his paperwork. "I just like your project."

By seven o' clock, show time, it appeared to everyone present that this was going to be another flop[121]. As Candace, her husband, and two of her friends waited for the concert to begin, Jim approached, running his fingers through his hair. "I don't know what to say! I'm embarrassed no one's here. I had this advertised on the radio all last week, on the web, here in the store…I mean, it's not as if you have a *bad* reputation."

"Well, but I have *no* reputation," I said. "That's the thing of it."

---

121 http://dissonantstates.com/post/12248459658/californiafragment

Just then, an older man with a motorcycle helmet walked through the door and found a seat. I was flooded with relief. At last, we had someone not affiliated with my sister or the space. "I know that guy," Jim said with a smile and a nudge. "Earlier today, I told him he had to come."

MAUI, HAWAII

I can't deny that music, the piano, my own efforts in America 88x50, have actually brought me here to Hawaii for the first time in my life; that because I play the piano, I'm on Maui, splayed out on the warm white sand of Baldwin Beach[122], intermittently diving into the water and letting the waves pull and push me out toward the breakers, then back toward shore. Since I was a kid, I always liked lying in the surf, lifeless like a corpse, just to see what it would feel like to let nature toss my body around like an object. To give up. To submit.

In my rented white Neon, I drove up a one-lane snake of a road connecting Wailuku, at sea level, to Studio Maluhia, a sleek, modern house which doubled as a concert space, perched on a mountainside and overlooking the ocean. It was surrounded by steep cliffs and distant waterfalls[123] and had a pool with a smooth, silent waterfall spilling off one end and a hot tub on

---

122 http://media.dissonantstates.com/i/BaldwinBeach.jpg

123 http://media.dissonantstates.com/i/MaluhiaWaterfall.jpg

the other. In what could only be described as Maluhia's living room[124], there was a concert grand Steinway and a majestic digital organ[125] front and center. It featured speakers lining the walls, sixteen in all, and a million stops and pedals. I was told it was the third largest organ in all of Hawaii.

Jack lived here. A computer tycoon and concert organist who split his time between San Francisco and Hawaii, he hoped that Maluhia would eventually develop into a busier venue, or a more prosperous one, perhaps with its own in-house ensemble performing for tourists wandering around Maui from cruise ships. As it stood now, though, he confessed that Maluhia was barely kept afloat by his efforts. As we talked, a helicopter flew by, filled with tourists.

Jack was having dinner with friends elsewhere on the island and wouldn't return until the next morning. I had Maluhia to myself for the night. Practicing, I kept my eyes focused ahead on the strings of the piano. Eating, I kept my eyes glued to my food. I wanted to look anywhere but into those dark windows that seemed so big, that seemed to be everywhere. Wind and rain began to howl and patter them, and little droplets turned into rivers, and they flowed down the windows like tears. I crept about the house, my heart jumping with every gust, every heavy sheet of rain, every creak in the walls. I kept thinking Jack was home, or that some ancient ghost had returned to take its revenge.

So I retreated to his computer and began chatting with locals, which of course yielded nothing, being

---

124 http://media.dissonantstates.com/i/Maluhia.jpg

125 http://media.dissonantstates.com/i/MaluhiaOrgan.jpg

that I was on top of a mountain. But of course I wasn't really looking for an actual companion anyway, rather a distraction, a search, a connection of some kind. How boring and endless, I thought, and the reality of just how boring and endless it all was came crushing down on me in an instant. *I could be doing this the rest of my life.* I shut down the computer and returned to the piano. Sitting on the bench, I was no longer afraid to look into the darkness of the wall-length windows beside me, streaming with its tiny rivers of rain. I stared straight into the black void and realized my reflection was crying too.

The next day, my audience sat in couches and folding lawn chairs scattered about the room, about sixty people in all. They applauded with zeal between each piece. The flashy Griffes *Sonata*[126] was so well received that I didn't know quite what to do, standing sweaty and grateful and puzzled before them, bowing over and over. When the concert ended, they all stood, clapping and shouting. These people had climbed up a one-lane road[127] hugging a mountainside to gather here in this house hanging off a cliff, and it was all to hear modern American music. At times like these, America 88x50 blossomed like a flower that only blooms on certain days and at a certain hour. Many people bought CDs and, as I was getting used to, asked me to sign them. Such was the faith of certain people that I would eventually make a gigantic splash with

---

126 http://media.dissonantstates.com/a/SonataHawaii.mp3

127 http://media.dissonantstates.com/i/RoadToMaluhia.jpg

America 88x50 and that they'd someday get to say that they "knew me when." Their words, not mine. But I was on state thirty-one and running out of time to, as CJ put it in Bozeman, "get discovered."

Jack appeared and gave me a hug. We promised to keep in touch, and said we hoped our paths would cross again. He stood back and began to nod his head. "You... you have a gift. The music comes out like poetry. And I prefer poetry to speeches."

"That's really nice of you to say."

"No," he retorted. "I don't just say things like that."

"This..." I gestured around the room, "has been incredible." But I began to shake my head now, my chest heaving slowly, tremors behind my eyes. Why was this happening? Why was I about to cry again?

"God is leading you on this journey," Jack said. There was a pause, a moment of gridlock. "He's leading you on this journey," he repeated.

"I'm glad you think so."

I never heard from Jack after I left Hawaii, but received an e-mail from my presenter some time later reporting that soon after my visit he had to sell the piano, the organ, and the house containing them. Studio Maluhia was gone. The e-mail closed with other news: *Funding is shrinking, along with the number of reasonable venues, newspaper coverage, etc. But audience size is greater than ever.*

JUNEAU, ALASKA

Touching down in Ketchikan, someone tells me I'm in the wrong seat. Moving a row ahead, I'm next to a young couple. She looks quite plain; he has tattoos everywhere. They were just married. He grew up in Spokane, but he calls it "Spoke-*can't.*"

"I have a friend from Spokane," I say.

She turns to me. "So your name is Adam?"

"Yes." Had I told her that?

"Adam...Tendler?"

I search my body for any indication as to why she would know my name. "I do graphic design," she explains, "and I help design the newsletter for the Juneau Arts Council. I think I worked on the poster for your concert."

"Wow! Small world!" I say, exhilarated.

"Small town," her husband corrects.

My presenters in Juneau, just like in Maui, volunteered to pay me. The rule in America 88x50 was simply that I would never *ask* for a fee, but I wouldn't turn it away if offered. After all, I had no funding and needed to get from place to place. The money from Alaska and Hawaii—I'd make $1,500 from Alaska, and I think my earnings from Hawaii totaled about the same—would help with my respective airfares and all the other tour expenses once I hit mainland again, or "outside," as they called it up here. Tickets for my show in Juneau, at the University of Alaska, ran for fifteen and twelve dollars, and posters designed by my friend from the plane were hanging in most of the windows around town. My first day there, I wandered wide-eyed around the streets[128] of

_____

128 http://media.dissonantstates.com/i/JuneauStreets.jpg

Juneau, a town landlocked between a dark channel of calm seawater and peaks[129] so tall and inexplicably close that they nearly curled over the roofs. The air smelled clean and wet. There was a glacier only miles away, melting faster and faster with each year, so they said, and all the mountains were peppered with dark pine trees, exposed cliffs, and patches of snow. Locals told me that wild bears sometimes crawled into town. Others warned me of avalanches.

Yes, I was in Alaska. Flying there[130] had happened so fast and easily that the reality of where I was kept registering at different times, like when I saw a license plate or a sign on a store. *Alaska.* In a way, I sort of missed traveling to places in my car. It made my destinations a little harder to get to, which made them, I don't know, I guess a little more real.

Thick snow fell like cotton balls outside as I sat in the studio of Juneau's public radio station with headphones on my ears, serving as a co-host for a weekly classical music program and discussing the tour with the show's regular hosts, a married couple. We were playing pieces by the composers from my program, bantering about twentieth-century music, giving away free tickets to my concert—callers had to answer trivia questions that we made up on the spot—and laughing on air at my own promo featuring an announcer describing America 88x50 while music from my CD played

129 http://media.dissonantstates.com/i/JuneauPeaks.jpg

130 http://dissonantstates.com/post/12334664744/alaskafragment

in the background. And in one of these exchanges, I referred to the music of my program as "honest," venturing to say that I thought bad modern art was out there, and that the layman—that exotic specimen—could indeed tell the difference between the good and the bad. In other words, even a non-specialist could distinguish between art which was honestly conceived and that which was produced solely for attention, for shock value. There could be some overlap, and sure, even some music on my program had elements of shock, but if a piece lacked that solid intention—call it heart, call it honesty, call it whatever—I argued that people, whether experienced listeners or not, would ultimately pick up on it.

Who determines a work's posterity? I was asked that by Mike in Hope, Arkansas. Now, half a year later, I thought I knew the answer: the public. But that doesn't mean the music needs to be watered down. Just well done.

The phone lit up. A woman wanted to speak with me. She ran a contemporary music festival in Juneau and wanted to invite me to a party the next night.

"Great radio show last night," a guy said to me in the crowded apartment, lit by small lamps and candles, with books and wine bottles and half-filled glasses everywhere.

"Thank you," I said. Most of the party's guests had heard about the tour, and they all seemed interested in talking to me about it, just as interested as the high school students I worked with that morning and the man who took me exploring in Glacier National Park earlier that afternoon—yes, it *was* melting[131]—and Madeline, who stood next to me, her brown hair pulled back tight in a hair tie, watched as I told stories to these guests about my travels. Then she spoke. "I think you need to be more careful with what you say on the radio."

There was silence.

"What?"

"You're only here for a couple days, but little things you say could be dangerous for contemporary music festivals like mine after you leave. When you say that people can tell the difference between good and bad modern music, you prepare people who simply *don't know it* to dislike it."

"Or invite people who don't know it into the dialogue," I said. "They should show up, listen, and decide for themselves."

"But who are you to blame the composer if they don't like it?"

"Should we blame the audience?"

So now it was getting a little awkward.

"I guess I just don't really believe in such a thing as a lay audience anymore," I said. "At least I stopped believing in it since I started this tour. Modern music can be engaging, depending on the idea that created it and how it's framed for an audience. In my shows, I talk a tiny bit about all of my pieces, and just that alone helps people appreciate it."

"Well, let's not get into that," she answered. "You're not really playing modern music. You're playing *Copland*."

---

131 http://media.dissonantstates.com/i/GlacierMelting.jpg

Now people began fanning away from us.

"*You* need to find *your* direction and choose the path *you're* going to take," she said. "I mean, are you a pianist or a composer or a presenter, or…"

Either this question was very fair or extremely unfair; I couldn't tell because I'd probably asked myself the same thing a million times. "I don't know," I answered.

"You need to choose."

"For…?"

"For people who will give you *money!*" she cried. "In the arts, you need to get grants and sponsors. This tour is nice, but what will you do when it's over?"

I barely had a clue what I would do after Alaska. "I don't know," I said again.

"Well, no one will ever take you seriously if you don't know what you want or who you are."

By now I wanted nothing more than to languish back at the Driftwood Lodge and sleep off whatever Madeline had re-awakened in me—that deep feeling of doubt, that urgent sensation of needing to change everything at once, to take action in all aspects of my life, and it didn't matter that I was traveling the country performing a tour which—thank you very much—was functioning with no grants or sponsors whatsoever, or that I'd gone from deep closet in June to having spent a week with a lover in Reno in November—all of this was still too undefined and unfocused and unfinished. I was, after all, still playing to empty halls. I was, after all, still in the closet. My journey to self-actualization had, so far, been totally half-assed. She was right.

A couple days later, Madeline came to the second of my two concerts at the University of Alaska and found me after the show. We hugged a long, knowing hug, and then she stepped back, looking sort of shaken. "The Copland," she said. "It's really something."

SEATTLE, WASHINGTON

Weaving through a redwood forest, passing attractions like "Confusion Mountain" and dodging lumber trucks with their fresh harvests of slaughtered trees stacked on their backs, I burst onto the coastline, waves crashing against the rocks, mist pink in the sunset, and I opened the sunroof to smell the seawater.

Since my tour depended largely on the kindness of strangers, I found myself thinking a lot about karma, so when I passed a hitchhiker a few miles later, I thought it might be a pretty good investment for me to stop and let him in. He wasn't very old, had a red beard, and wore a puffy purple jacket that invaded even into the driver's side. He lodged his giant red backpack between the dashboard and his knees. "I was freaking out back there, dude," he said. "It's getting dark and there's no place to stay in any of these one-horse towns." He said that he'd started hitchhiking the day before in Santa Rosa, and wanted me to drop him off in Crescent City, a town right around the California and Oregon border. I asked why he left Santa Rosa, and he said he'd had issues with his girlfriend. "I have family in Crescent City and can start over there." He sniffled. "You know, on the East Coast people stop for hitchhikers a lot more. Last year it took me only one day to get from Florida to New Jersey, and I've been out here since six o' clock yesterday morning and, what—Santa Rosa's like three or four hours away?"

I actually had no idea where Santa Rosa was, even though apparently I'd driven through it earlier that day. Anyway, I was still digging for stories. What happened with his girlfriend? Did drivers ever hit on him? Or did they get paranoid and ask him to empty his pockets? I was projecting in every direction. "I'm the one who shouldn't trust people!" he retorted, legs shaking, his eyes staring out into the darkness. "Some guy drove off with my other bag yesterday, the one I had all my clothes and my ID in."

So what was in that red backpack then? It was so full that the zippers seemed about ready to burst. And who would ever put their ID in their bag?

"When do you think I should cut over to the 5 from the 101?" I asked.

"Cop."

"What?"

"Cop, dude. *Right there!*" He pointed to the side of the road, but I still couldn't see anything, squinting through my glasses. But then there it was, a dark clump of a patrol car hidden in the bushes, and even as I pressed the brakes, I could already see its tires begin to roll onto the highway as we dashed by.

The car swept onto the highway behind us and sped up until it was nearly against my back bumper. We went for about a half-mile like this, breathless, without words, and then the lights began. Then a siren.

"Fuck," I said.

"Dude, I don't have any ID!" he repeated, trembling. I started pulling over. "And where's th—the seatbelt?

My seatbelt's not on! Dude, where's the *seatbelt?*" As he struggled to find it, I stopped the car and the officer approached the passenger side window. "*I can't roll down the fucking window! Dude! How the fuck do I—*"

There was a tap on the window next to his face, and the hitchhiker froze. I pressed a button on my door to roll the passenger window down, noticing that his left hand was holding the seatbelt against his hip. He'd been too terrified to find the buckle.

"How you two doing tonight?" the officer asked, bending over to bring his head level with the passenger window. "I stopped you because you were going seventy-eight and this *is*," he emphasized, "a fifty-five-mile-per-hour zone. When it cuts back to one lane in each direction, it becomes fifty-five again." I nodded. He looked at my license. "I take it this is your current address." He said it more like a statement than a question, and then disappeared out of sight. In the rearview, I saw him back in the squad car, writing.

"Goddamn it," I said. The hitchhiker was still twitching in his seat, still panting, still clutching the seatbelt against his waist. "This is my fourth fucking ticket in five months. First Missouri, then Wyoming, then Kansas. Now here. And what's funny is that before my tour, I used to get out of *every* ticket whenever I'd get pulled over. I once ran a red light and almost crashed into a police car—no ticket. I once *fled* from a police car by driving the *wrong way* down a *one-way street* as he trailed behind me, and—you guessed it—no ticket! Talk about karma! This is karma catching up with m—"

"He's taking pretty long," the hitchhiker interrupted. "Why, do you think?"

"Here he comes."

The officer returned, this time to my window, and said that as a "favor" he cut my speed down from seventy-eight to just seventy so that I wouldn't have to pay a nearly three-hundred-dollar fine. He wished us a pleasant drive and watched as I crawled back onto the 101. The hitchhiker sighed in relief, releasing the seat belt from his hip.

"I guess it could have been worse," I said.

"Yes, *much* worse," he said, and then muttered something while eyeing his bag. I thought I heard the word "kilo."

"What?"

"Listen, there's a Walmart in Crescent City where you can drop me off. I'll wait there for...um, my family."

Waiting for service to begin in a pew of the Episcopalian Church of St. John the Baptist in southwest Seattle, I stared up at Jesus, floating[132] in front of a cross that hung above the altar—not nailed, just floating, with his arms raised. His expression looked more pained and pathetic than I'd ever seen before, a grimace almost too gruesome to look at. I felt a hand on my shoulder and jumped in my seat.

"Hey, buddy."

That soft, scratchy voice—Shane. He came. He really came. "You came!"

"It's not that bad of a drive from Spokane. I really wanted to see you play your concert."

---

132 http://media.dissonantstates.com/i/JesusPiano.jpg

"It's not till three," I said.

"Well, I go to church every Sunday anyway, so I came to this one today hoping you'd be here already. And look! Here you are!"

"Who are you staying with?"

"My aunt. How have you been?"

"I've missed you."

"Me too, buddy."

It felt like weeks since we last talked. He'd begun interviewing for a new job as a guard at a youth detention center, and I'd been so overwhelmed with Hawaii and Alaska that it had become easier not to think of him, everything about him, but in this moment, I wanted nothing more than to jump up and embrace him, kiss him, love him. But there was a sweet kind of agony in not being able to show even a fraction of what we wanted to show each other there in that church, and we were content to just smile and smolder inside.

"What's that behind him?" I asked, pointing discreetly to what looked like wings hovering behind the back of Jesus.

"That's a cape," he said, his blue eyes glistening as he looked up.

"Jesus had a cape?"

"It's meant to glorify him," he whispered back. "It's symbolic."

The service began. Shane sat down and pointed to the note about my recital in the announcements section of the worship program. I nodded. "Was it advertised anywhere else?" he whispered. I shook my head no.

Then he pulled out from the hymnal rack a small red offertory envelope made of construction paper, on which it appeared a child had scrawled a message in pencil:

if you are reading this you will die when you get home

I hear a shuffling in the back of the room, doors creaking open and slamming shut, wet shoes squeaking against the floor. In the blizzard of notes that comprise the Griffes *Sonata* finale, I turn and see Peter, the pastor, sitting in the very last pew with an African American family. The family is soaked, their rain gear glistening and dripping. I suddenly remember that this concert is a benefit, and that the family I'm seeing was displaced by Hurricane Katrina. I have roughly twenty people in my audience, and wonder how much money we've raised.

Peter and his wife took Shane and me out for dinner that night. Instantly charmed by his friendly disposition and interested in his church upbringing, they talked mostly to Shane as I stared out at the Seattle skyline, bright and green against the Pacific night, which was fine with me. Finally, I interrupted. "Peter, that family you were sitting with…"

"That's the family our church is hosting, the family who lost everything in Katrina. Habitat for Humanity, who received all the proceeds from your concert tonight, is building a house for them." I sighed. He could tell what I was thinking. "Listen, it's not about how much money we raised. What you said about how audiences might hear the music of America 88x50 differently after Katrina...the father looked at me and," Peter tried to find the words, "and it was like you spoke directly to his heart."

"Really?"

"Your program made perfect sense to all of them."

Peter and his wife invited Shane and me to stay at their home that night. I would sleep on a twin bed in their guest room, and they would drag in a futon for Shane. That was the plan, at least, but once we all said goodnight and the house went dark, he slipped out from under his blankets and climbed into my little bed, his head on my pillow, back against my chest, and I clutched him close, kissing his neck, his ears, his shoulders, pulling him closer and closer until there was no him and me anymore.

The next morning, before we said goodbye at a nearby gas station—and I snapped a photo of him[133] in the parking lot, not knowing if or when I'd see him again—we all four had breakfast at the house. I wondered if Peter and his wife suspected anything about Shane and me. They had to know, right? And then the strangest thing happened. A feeling came over me, or rather, a non-feeling. For once, and maybe for the first time ever, I actually didn't care.

CORVALLIS, OREGON

Apparently there's a town-wide ordinance that has banned anyone from getting married in Corvallis until

---

133 http://media.dissonantstates.com/i/ShaneParkingLot.jpg

gays and lesbians can marry too. Outside the Church of the Good Samaritan, a banner reads: CONCERT THIS SUNDAY. Fantastic, but my concert is Tuesday— tomorrow—and I'm concerned. My host explains that the church has only one banner for their concert series, which evidently is a *Sunday* concert series.

"But people will know," he assures. "It's in the bulletin."

"Have you ever had a concert on a Tuesday before?" I ask.

"No."

I visited a local CD store. A man with glasses and a ponytail noticed me browsing and asked, "You moving here as a student?"

"No, I'm playing piano recitals of modern American music in all fifty states, and tomorrow I'm playing the Oregon concert here in Corvallis." It was so automatic by now; just fill in the blank with city and state. As he asked more and more questions and grew increasingly fascinated and enthusiastic, at one point taking notes, the more I felt like I was fulfilling a duty for grassroots audience development. What I liked most of all was seeing this man, so outside the classical music sphere, captivated by the project. He and his friends, and the students of the university that defined this town, were all the people who I wanted sitting in the audience at an America 88x50 concert.

Of course, none of them actually came, but still, a couple dozen other people did—they must have read the bulletin—and they loved it. The question of whether these regular attendees of the Good Samaritan Church concert series would have attended *any* show, regardless of whether I was performing modern American music or juggling scarves for an hour and a half, was insignificant to me. I was just happy they came. I did my job. Checked off my state. Made a little cash. And now it was time to head back east, making a couple stops along the way, just hoping that everything would continue as smoothly as it had for the past couple of states. It was as if I was waiting for something to go horribly wrong.

INTERLUDE: SUPAI

After my high school army-tent tryst with Calvin, we still saw each other, but only so often, and usually in odd places. Sometimes in the Toyota truck I drove throughout high school. Sometimes at my house. Once on a baseball field, where we finished in the dugout. Or in his room, where I also learned about his experiences, his family, his past, his pains, his travels. And all through it I was, as far as I could tell, falling in love. The first time.

And one night he showed me a photo album of a place in Arizona he'd visited, a place that changed his life. It was this oasis in the middle of the desert, miles from civilization, where there were aqua waterfalls cascading into crystal-clear pools, surrounded by lush green trees and towering red boulders. It was a reservation for the Havasupai Indians, and on the map, it was just a dot marked "Supai" with no roads attached to it.

☆

The ghost of whatever Calvin and I had shared and lost back in high school accompanied me all the way through college, all the way through America 88x50, and all the way to Arizona between my Oregon and Kansas shows. I told myself that I simply owed this trip to myself, that indeed I had been captivated by those pictures in his photo album and that I did want to experience this secret fountain of youth deep in the Grand Canyon, because when else would I have the chance? But even through the haze of competing rationalizations, there was this feeling that I'd be closer to Calvin down there in Supai, closer than I'd ever been before, and that maybe then I'd be closer to putting that ghost of us to rest, to putting him behind me.

I tore south through California and hooked east onto Route 66 into an enveloping desert, fixed on my destination with my mind both racing and blank, as if I was going to a class reunion with no idea of what I'd do or say once I got there. At one point I shook a bottle of chocolate milk that I'd bought at a truck stop, realizing only after showering everything inside the car in brown, dripping suds, that I'd already removed the cap.

It's around sixty miles between Kingman, the nearest city to Supai, and Supai Junction, which is nothing more than a discreet turnoff. Then it's about another sixty or so miles down that narrow road, with signposts marking every excruciating mile, to the parking area. That's where people begin their hikes. It was late morning and I had a simple plan. I'd arrive, hike in, see the waterfalls, maybe jump into the water—I wore swimming trunks under my jeans—and then I'd return to the car and continue my drive, probably stopping in Albuquerque that night to sleep, and then on to Kansas for my next concert, slotted for a few days later. Simple!

The road straightened out to reveal what looked like a secret trap door of a canyon's edge[134], a chasm the bottom of which I couldn't see, abrupt and frightfully close. I gasped. The massive geometry of this place, the walls of sandy rock, the gorges splitting the earth just a few meters from my Hyundai, extending as far as I could see; I felt privileged to witness it, and stopped the car[135] to stand alone on the canyon's edge.

I hadn't seen a single car since Supai Junction, and drove up a little further to the parking lot, which was full, but still no people. They probably can't tear themselves away from the waterfalls, I thought, and just then, a hot gust of wind cut against my skin. I decided to put a sweater on under my jean jacket, stuffing a few Dr. Peppers in its pockets to enjoy by the water once I got there. I nestled on my favorite John Deer hat, left my cell phone in the car, and headed to the path.

Two girls climbed up onto the trailhead[136]. Finally, a sign of life! They looked sweaty, exhausted, and out of breath, each hauling a large backpack dangling with tents and sleeping pads. Why all the fuss? I thought. I'm a Vermonter. A hike like this is nothing. I smiled and brushed by them.

---

134 http://media.dissonantstates.com/i/SupaiCanyon.jpg

135 http://media.dissonantstates.com/i/SupaiHyundai.jpg

136 http://media.dissonantstates.com/i/SupaiTrailhead.jpg

Skidding down a rock path just wide enough for my feet, I gradually made it to the canyon bottom. Once there, I stopped and turned around 360 degrees, taking in the sprawl and sizzle of this valley. I couldn't hear any waterfalls, though. Maybe they were hiding behind one of those canyon walls[137].

Did I lock my car? Of course I did. I had to have. I walked on, concentrating mostly on balance and footing; I was wearing new Adidas sneakers with barely any tread, and was sliding around the path as if I had skis on. After about two hours and several more people schlepping by from the opposite direction, all of them elaborately decorated with gear, I finally stopped two women. "Is it a far way down?"

"Let me think," one of them answered, looking at her watch. A ball of sweat dripped down her cheek from behind her sunglasses like a teardrop. "We started at," she looked at her companion, "what do you think, quarter to ten? Yeah, about nine forty-five we left."

"And what time is it now?" I asked, realizing that I'd left my main timekeeping device, my phone, in the car with my other timekeeping device, my laptop. Did I lock my car?

"It's about one-fifteen," she answered.

"Okay," I said with some delight. "So, in three-and-a-half-hours I'll be back here, in this spot?" I just wanted to confirm.

She laughed. "No!" And then she paused, almost waiting for me to laugh, too. "Wait, are you serious? It's three-and-a-half hours till you get to the village. And the falls are several miles further down from there."

---

137 http://media.dissonantstates.com/i/SupaiExpanse.jpg

A terrified smile stayed frozen on my face.

"It's an eight-mile hike," she said. "You are spending the night, right?"

"I, um...I guess so!"

She gave me a mildly distressed, sympathetic look, and continued walking. Crestfallen, I weighed my options. I could hike back to the car, which would take at least a couple hours, and then it would be another few hours to reach an interstate, and then it would take all night to get to New Mexico. Safe and sensible, yes, but also a complete resignation, a waste of a day, a defeat. The other option was to keep walking—no colitis meds, nowhere to put my contact lenses, no glasses to replace them in case they ripped or dried or fell out, and no idea of when or where I would eat or sleep that night. What I did have was a credit card, two Dr. Peppers, and a couple dollars in cash. The rest of my money was in the console of the car. Did I lock the car?

I decided to continue onward. My mouth instantly began to feel dry and I could already feel the muscles in my legs struggling to keep up with the pace of my feet, tripping and bumping over the rocks, sinking into the loose gravel and silky sands of the dried riverbed that made up the path to Supai. I kept my eyes focused on the ground, rarely glancing up. If I looked up[138], I would fall.

After what felt like a few more hours, I asked another group of campers making their exit how much longer I had to go. "Probably two or so hours," said one girl with a smile, her wet face covered with dust.

---

138 http://media.dissonantstates.com/i/SupaiRedRock.jpg

Her companion—he had a beard and wore wire-rimmed glasses—rose to his feet. "No! No, no...at least three and a half. Probably four!"

"Oh, my God," I said. "I really underestimated this. Is it crowded down there?"

"The campground has a ton of room," she said. "I'm sure the lodge does, too."

"Lodge?"

"Yes," her gloomy companion answered. "It'll run you about one twenty-five." He turned to me and groaned, "Do you have enough water?" He seemed almost offended at how ridiculously unprepared I was for this hike.

I laughed back. "It's fine, thanks. I have two Dr. Peppers. Does the lodge take Visa?"

Finally, hours later, I could hear running water. And then I saw it[139], a small stream running thick and steady, bright blue, the same kind of water I saw in Calvin's photo album. Yes, it looked exactly the same! I stepped to the stream and dipped my hand into it, expecting an icy shock that would chill me to the core. Instead, it was exquisitely warm and soft. I splashed it across my face and tasted sweat and dirt dripping from my forehead and cheeks.

The village[140] came slowly, at first only trailers and doublewides spaced far apart and always surrounded by tattered cattle[141] pens with one or two animals slowly stalking around inside. The homes looked as if their inhabitants had long vacated them, and I considered

139 http://media.dissonantstates.com/i/SupaiWater.jpg
140 http://media.dissonantstates.com/i/SupaiVillageSign.jpg
141 http://media.dissonantstates.com/i/SupaiCattle.jpg

sneaking into one of them to sleep that night if the lodge was full. When I finally stumbled into the center of town, I found there was a little grocery store, a small post office, a diner, and a church[142] in the shape of a half-moon made of sheet metal. And then, of course, there was the lodge, which looked surprisingly modern, like any motel. I'd never worked so hard to get away from civilization in my life, and suddenly I was in a town. Before walking into the lodge, I went to the store and procured a Snickers bar, a postcard, and some saline solution for my contacts. They only accepted cash, and after my purchase I had three dollars left in my wallet.

At the front desk of the lodge, I gratefully handed over my Visa card—thank God *they* took plastic—as a helicopter took off from the town square in a choppy, dusty mess. A suburban-looking white woman appeared beside me and asked the receptionist, sort of in a panic, "What is that helicopter for?"

"Tourists."

"Will…will there be another today?"

"It's for tourists," she repeated, and turned her back to both of us.

"But will there be another, or was that the last one?" asked the woman again, now speaking directly to the back of the receptionist's head, into her braided black hair.

"I don't know," said the braid, and that was that. The suburban woman vanished out the door.

I asked the braid how to make a phone call, and it said three dollars. Then she spun around and collected the last remaining bills I had in my wallet.

---

142 http://media.dissonantstates.com/i/SupaiChurch.jpg

"Is your car locked?" asked my mom through the phone receiver.

My heart sank again. I'd nearly forgotten that I was worried about this. "I think so," I said, fondling the dirty telephone cord. "Anyway, I really should go."

"Okay, honey…I'm glad you called. Oh, my God."

"Oh, my God?"

"What?"

"You said 'Oh, my God.'"

"I did? Well…" she chuckled, still sounding very anxious, "maybe it's just because in all your travels, you've never once called me to say you've arrived somewhere, no matter how many times I've asked you to. So you're calling now, it seems, because you want me to know where you are. Like you think you might not make it back."

About a mile and a half past the village, I stood at the edge of the water, watching it bubbling and glowing[143]. It was dusk. Vines hung from surrounding rocks and water shot from holes in the mountainside.

I tore off my clothes and jumped into the water[144], feeling leaves and debris nipping and brushing at my toes like little minnows. The water felt colder now, but healing, and when I emerged shortly afterward, my legs no longer throbbed.

But I was shivering—I had no towel—and I ran back to the village shirtless, with my sweater and jeans in hand.

143 http://media.dissonantstates.com/i/SupaiPool.jpg
144 http://media.dissonantstates.com/i/SupaiPool2.jpg

Once back in my room, I realized that I wouldn't have any time the next day to see any other falls. I needed to get back to the car and on my way. So this was it. I saw all I'd probably ever see of the Supai waterfalls.

☆

I felt a terrible pain, like something had been ripped or severed inside my left kneecap, and I couldn't straighten my leg without this pain shooting up and completely debilitating my brain and body. My contacts were dirtier than they'd ever been, and I had them in a paper cup filled with the sterile eye solution I'd bought at the store. Dirt and debris collected at the bottom of the cup.

I couldn't take a full breath without coughing.

That night I didn't sleep as much as I dreamed, and these dreams were mostly of blank score paper filling up with scribbled music, like an animation, music full of dissonant counterpoint and un-resolvable cadences. In other moments, I laid there awake in disbelief. I couldn't believe I'd come here and what a disaster it had all turned into. And then I'd think that it served me right. All this for Calvin?

Purple shadows appeared outside my window and dim traces of sun hit my curtains. I decided to stand up and prepare to leave, but nearly fell down beside the bed. My left knee was destroyed. I could barely walk across the room. I made it to the bathroom counter and tried putting in my contact lenses, but they burned so badly I had to take them out. Even with them out, my eyes still seared with pain and were spilling tears, streaking my red, dirty face. I was blind. I was hyperventilating. I would have to hike out of Supai with no vision and one leg.

I hopped on my good leg out of the room into the cold, blue desert morning, easing myself down the balcony stairs to ground level. A few paces away, my left leg straightened and touched the ground, a fatal error that pinched the nerves inside my kneecap so painfully that I shouted, "Holy fuck!" and stood still, looking around desperately, panting, truly scared. I stepped down again, kind of testing to see if this would happen again, and it did, the internal sting shooting from my knee up through my entire body. *I can't do this*, I thought. Then I said it out loud. "You can't do this." Ice-cold beads of sweat formed on my head. "You can't do this. You can't do this."

A few tourists walked by. "Hello. Hello," I said, trying to smile, wincing. "Good morning. Yes, everything's fine! I'm fine!"

They walked on, and once alone again, I assessed the situation and created a mode of operation. I would step and plant my right leg, and then drag my bent left leg to meet it. Step. Plant. Drag. It was my only option. I *could* do this. I had to do this.

It took me what seemed like an eternity to traverse, like a zombie, that same expanse of rocky canyons and open desert and vertical cliff faces out of Supai. Many times my useless sandpaper eyes would lead me off the blurry path and into a dead end, where I'd feel around the rocks with my hands like a blind person, then look upward for some moving body or shadow that might help point me back to the path, and then I'd drag myself on course. No Dr. Peppers left, I found an abandoned, half-full bottle of water near the final cliff ascent. I guzzled its contents, letting it overflow and stream down my chest. Then I dragged myself up the canyon wall, step by step, drag by drag, and once ascended, fell onto the hood of my Hyundai. It had been locked the whole time.

I could have cried for the pain, for the gratitude, for the embarrassment of having come here, my stupid motivations. Coughing—I couldn't stop coughing—I got into the car, revved the accelerator, and took off without stopping until I reached civilization. At the first mailbox I saw, I stopped the car and reached into my pocket, taking out the crinkled postcard I'd purchased at the Supai grocery—a picture of a waterfall which of course I never saw—and scrawled an address I couldn't believe I still had memorized. Calvin's parents' house. I didn't know where he was, but somehow knew he'd get it.

I could only think of two words to write on the postcard, and hobbled out of the car to toss it and everything I'd ever associated with it, with him, with Supai, away into the mailbox.

FINALLY WENT.

SALINA, KANSAS

If I took anything deeper than a quick, surface breath, an awful tickle in my chest would explode into a fit of coughs, with green globs of phlegm splattering out of my mouth. My body ached from the inside out, and my skin was sensitive to the touch of my clothes, the air, water, anything. After just a few steps, I had to rest. It was like the dust and sand of the desert was still in my veins, and my body wouldn't be free from it until the desert was good and ready to let me go.

Sick as I felt, though, I still came very close to meeting another online phantom. With Shane in another time zone, he might as well have been in another galaxy. This man lived in Oklahoma City, my stopping point between Arizona and Kansas. So there I was, on the same day that I'd hiked out of the Grand Canyon, circling the northwest loop of Oklahoma City, looking for some shopping mall parking lot where this guy said he would wait. Hacking, sneezing, and battling to keep my eyes open, I found the parking lot, but he wasn't there, nor was he answering my texts or phone calls. I was in no shape to meet anyone for anything, but it bothered me that he'd just vanished like that. It hurt.

But part of me wondered if I just came here to *confirm* that it was bullshit to begin with. Perhaps this was how I worked in general, and my life was one long string of bullshit confirmations; in America 88x50, setting the bar higher and higher just to confirm in time that the tour was meant to fail, or asking myself onstage about the notes in the next measures just so I could eventually forget them, or wearing patent leather to my eighth-grade graduation just so the other kids could call me a faggot, or, at seven years old, asking my father during his weekend visits if he smoked just so I could watch him lie and say he didn't.

I *knew* he smoked. I'd seen him do it. And if he went into the store and came back with a bag of groceries, I'd climb into the backseat and find the cigarettes hiding at the bottom of the bag. But then I'd simply go on with my day, satisfied with my bullshit confirmation. I'd never pull out the cigarettes and confront him. I didn't want to humiliate my father. I just wanted one time to see if he'd prove me wrong, tell me the truth, and just say yes.

So this was how I worked, I realized in Oklahoma City.

It was the first day of December, and the thin, freezing air took my breath away as I struggled out of the Hyundai in the back parking lot of the Stiefel Theatre and limped to the stage door. Audience chairs were set up on the stage[145] surrounding the piano, and there was a long curtain draped upstage against which blue and green stage lights shined, creating an ethereal effect which to me looked like being underwater. I was proud to be there; proud this was my show, still proud and amazed as ever to have my name up on the marquee outside[146].

I played for big butch Kansas men with their pleasant wives and quiet kids, a piano teacher with her students, a group of senior citizens, and a handful of high school students captured from my outreach performance the day before. A theater technician watched from offstage. My fingers felt crackly and stiff like tree bark, and my hands clunked around the keyboard as if I'd all but

145 http://media.dissonantstates.com/i/StiefelStage.jpg

146 http://media.dissonantstates.com/i/StiefelMarquee.jpg

forgotten its topography. But I had to truly believe and trust in the fact that it had only been a short period between Oregon and now, and that I *knew* the piano, and I *knew* this music, and that in order to survive on this stage I would need to turn off all the other noise in my head. And I did. Which meant, I *could*.

I could turn it off?

LINCOLN, NEBRASKA

Snowbound in a motel room, I can't breathe. I go to the emergency room. A doctor throws a prescription at me for some antibiotics and I skate away from the hospital on my summer tires.

Deb told me not to come to Lincoln. There was no way her arts council could host me with the holidays so close and on such short notice, and with all her other shows. But there I was, introducing myself in her doorway, watching her face turn a shade of surprise that I don't think I'll ever see again. She didn't turn me away, though. She said she'd think about what we could do, and in the meantime, I was to stalk around town looking for anywhere, any*one*, who could host the concert. So, like a traveling salesman, I walked around frozen Lincoln, pitching the concert, holding my breath as I spoke to keep from coughing. "I don't know what I'd do with any of *that!*" spat one piano storeowner.

The more I stared at my atlas, the more certain I grew that some way, somehow, I needed to create a show in

Lincoln that week. There was no way I could come all the way back out here to try again in the third leg of the tour. Deb saw my determination, or rather, that I wasn't going anywhere, and started calling any potential Lincoln hosts she could think of, and in the process got a firsthand dose of what it was like to propose America 88x50. I began to share her office[147], and would watch her hang up the phone and sit back in her office chair, shaking her fists into the air, shouting, "We just need one 'Yes!'"

Deb also knew I was hemorrhaging money on my motel room, and offered me her council's Artist in Residence apartment[148], a structure that used to be a public men's restroom standing in the front yard of City Hall. Inside was spacious, chic, with a living room, kitchen, and bedroom. I didn't have a show to speak of, but was officially Lincoln's newest Artist in Residence.

Finally, on a Monday, Union College agreed to host me that following Sunday, and Deb and I jumped around the room. By Tuesday, a series of e-mails about America 88x50 had circulated throughout town and posters were printed. I had a radio appearance booked, and a newspaper reporter planned to do a story about the show. The more Deb introduced me to people, the more it seemed they'd already heard about the concert. "Oh, so *you're* the pianist…"

It was Friday, and I was so cold, even indoors, that at all times I wore a winter coat and knit cap. I'd bought

147 http://dissonantstates.com/post/12790064043/balladofdeb

148 http://media.dissonantstates.com/i/LincolnApartment.jpg

the latter at a Walmart; it had an AC/DC logo on it. I felt like I could fall asleep at any second. I was still coughing. I'd had the hiccups for three days. The antibiotics had done nothing. After a nap that afternoon, I woke up almost completely unable to move my neck, and my head throbbed with every heartbeat. I rushed into the bathroom, and my stomach and colon tensed and spit out streams of diarrhea. Frightened for another colitis flare-up, I looked for blood. None. None yet.

Go back to the hospital? I had visions of my twenty-third birthday less than a year earlier, transferred as an emergency patient to New York's Mt. Sinai, with a biohazard sticker on my door because doctors thought maybe a parasite had triggered my colitis, nurses refusing to take a slice of my birthday cake when offered, me shuffling around in a hospital gown, pushing an IV drip on wheels, my mother beside me, quietly terrified at the sight of her young son as an old man.

But I went back, had an X-ray and a CAT scan, and a nurse administered an IV. I watched the needle enter my arm as a thin ribbon of blood sprayed across the room. "So what brings you to Lincoln?" she asked. Just then, a doctor entered the room and said I had mono, that he couldn't give me anything for it, and that I should go home to Vermont immediately. I stared at him and said only, "I can't."

☆

By now it's completely pointless to wonder about whether or not this is a good idea—it's not—so I labor to keep my sabotage-addicted brain on track.

The Aphex Twin opener sounds perfect, and the Ives shakes the room. When I finish and stand to bow, I nearly faint. I can't catch my breath, but still I introduce the Griffes with spurts of sentences between long pauses. During one such pause, someone farts loudly. After the Griffes and Ginastera, my clothes are sopping wet, and when I bow, I stay down, coughing with my face out of sight and the sound concealed by my audience applauding.

MADISON, WISCONSIN

It was a miracle he still spoke to me, Ben from Madison, who became my best friend at IU as quickly as he became…well, not quite an enemy, but part of a friendship that I had to destroy lest I myself become destroyed by it—by what I felt in it, which was much more than friendship.

From the day I first saw him at freshman orientation, when he stood up, announced that he played the trumpet, and promptly asked about intramural sports—and I groaned from six rows back—I always thought of him as the most unattainable and unlikely of friends, which of course made the challenge of befriending him, of possessing him, all the more appealing. He was handsome, talented, creative, personable, liberal, funny, repulsed by drugs and alcohol, and paralyzed by stage fright—one of the things we bonded over early on.

We were sophomores, roommates, and up to that point, inseparable, when he started dating a beautiful soprano, Rachel, a mutual friend of ours and another one of my favorite people at Indiana University. In an instant, I turned his and my friendship off. I stopped talking to Ben completely, and we'd fall asleep in opposite bunks wrapped in excruciating silence. Ben didn't know what had come over me, and I actually didn't know either. It was like my reasonable self had been taken hostage by some embarrassing, stifling addiction to prove some kind of point—indefensible and indefinable—because all we were ever supposed to be was friends. I couldn't bear to admit why I was hurt, not even to myself.

So I torched our relationship instead. We stopped living as roommates and saw each other only in passing. I thought he'd never forgive me—how could he?—but when I finally apologized later in the summer, he forgave me on the spot and required no explanation. Even in forgiveness, Ben was almost too perfect.

So I shouldn't have been surprised when Ben invited me to his family's home during the holiday season when I was sick and contagious with mono, seeing stars if I walked more than ten paces and only just getting over my Supai limp. Seeing him, still so handsome, standing in the doorway, I remembered that December evening two years earlier, when I stole away from Bloomington with no intention of ever looking back, and we sobbed in the college bookstore parking lot across from the music school—horns honking, people wanting my spot—and I sobbed all the way through Indiana, then Ohio, then all the way to a rest area near Buffalo, New York, where I fell out of my Chevy truck and shat blood all across the icy ground, unable to make it to the bathroom a few hundred feet away, a postcard from my incurable colitis, and how I crumbled there on the snowy pavement in a heap of tears, my waste steaming in red puddles around me. Yes, it all came back in an instant.

Over pancakes, Ben's father presents me with the arts section of the newspaper. I'm a "well-traveled clavierist" with "the heart of a roving folk singer" it says, and America 88x50 is picked as one of Madison's Best Bets for the weekend, printed with equal size and billing next to *The Nutcracker*. All of this I arranged from my sick bed in Lincoln.

Ben hadn't officially graduated from IU. He still needed to complete his senior recital and kept failing his hearings, just like I'd failed mine. Now living at home in Madison, the clock was ticking before his degree extension would expire, and by now he was so aggravated that he considered giving up altogether. He hadn't played the trumpet in weeks. We'd always shared our insecurities, so talking about them was strangely addictive for us, almost seductive, and as much as I wished we could help free each other of our hang-ups, there was also this question of what we'd have left to talk about if we did. Where would that bond go?

"You can start fresh," I said. We were in his bedroom, him on the top bunk and me on the bottom, where I spent most of my time in Madison, napping, resting, and recuperating as Ben and the rest of his family bustled about, preparing for the holidays. "You should view

this break as an opportunity. Maybe when you start playing again—say, after New Year's?—commit to *not* doing
anything you've ever done before. See what happens,
and at the next recital hearing just do your best." I
could hear him thinking. It was a familiar silence. Then
I heard him prop his body up, the bedsprings squeaking
and a magazine tumbling to his side.

"Of course I'll do my best. What does that mean?"

"Well, I'm just saying…"

"Do you think I wasn't trying to *do my best* when I
failed my last hearings? Were you not trying to *do your
best* when you failed yours?" I didn't say anything. "If you
don't complete the tour, will it be because you weren't
trying your best? Of course not. Everyone always *does
their best.*"

Now that he mentioned it, I wasn't so sure. Actually,
the longer we explored the subject, the more conceiv-
able it seemed that I'd never actually tried my best at
anything. Had I ever really practiced enough? Probably
not, and look at how I played. Was I really committing
enough energy to America 88x50? Probably not, and
look at the state of the tour—I had nothing planned for
the Gulf Coast, and America 88x50 was still invisible to
nearly everyone but my friends and a handful of audiences. But I didn't say anything. We were deadlocked,
like two wrestlers bonded and embraced in the first
couple seconds of their match, stopping each other
with equal, opposing force. Even after all these years
apart, we could return in an instant right to where we'd
left off.

☆

The Madison Center for Creative and Cultural Arts—MCCCA—was a small performing arts center standing literally in the shadow of The Overture Center, Madison's premiere venue, presenting *The Nutcracker* that night, my competition. Besides Ben's family, there was one mother and son who traveled over an hour to attend my recital, another girl who claimed to have been following America 88x50 for months—though I had no idea how—and one woman whose son, a young violist, was at home suffering from a physically debilitating disease. "Remember," she said, motioning to the crowd, "*we* are on your side. The only time an audience wants you to fail is in music school."

The director introduced me, using words like "courageous" and "disciplined," even "intellectual," and then spoke at length about the importance of arts advocacy, artistic perseverance, and creative conviction, all of which he said America 88x50 embodied. I smiled from the back of the room, feeling myself getting healthier, convinced that this was the perfect place for America 88x50. And it's a shame, considering that not long after I left Madison, MCCCA closed its doors permanently due to lack of funding.

☆

I hug Ben good-bye and walk out of his house into the bright winter morning. The glass door swings wildly on its hinges behind me before shutting with a bang. The street I drive away on is glassy with ice and, against my better judgment, I don't let up until Vermont, save for a few minutes curled up in the driver's seat at a rest stop near Buffalo.

NORTH CONWAY, NEW HAMPSHIRE

Mostly healed from the mono and with the holidays officially over—I presented my family with gifts from across
the country purchased with the cash of sympathetic
concertgoers—I had no excuse to not be back on the
phone, back in the saddle, back to begging people to
take me up on my fifty-state scavenger hunt for pianos
and audiences. I had thirteen states left and wanted to
wrap this all up by June, a year from when I started.
It wasn't lost on me that I was asking presenters for a
small miracle—most had their seasons planned for
years in advance, and here I wanted my shows booked
within weeks, days, hours—but I also knew I was asking for something, as unreasonable as it may have been,
that was still possible. If I'd proved anything in America
88x50, I proved that this was all possible.

I sat in the passenger seat looking out at a marshmal-
low landscape of two days' worth of snow, thinking several concerts ahead of the one I'd just played that evening in North Conway, a warm, inviting town sprouting
from a crack in the New Hampshire White Mountain
range. "During the potluck dinner after your concert,"
my mother said from the driver's seat, "one man from
the church called you a phenomenon. 'I just saw a musical phenomenon,' he said. And that's what people think
when they come to your concerts, that they're witness-
ing a phenomenon, that they're *part* of that phenomenon! But you seem unhappy tonight."

I couldn't argue, but I also wasn't armed with the
kind of honesty required to explain why. America 88x50
had activated an almost undetectable metamorphosis in

me since the day I started it over half a year earlier, and in living on the road with no one to answer to, I was granted exactly the kind of freedom I needed, which I never knew I needed. The freedom to express the most personal side of myself, which always happened at the piano, in the setting I felt safest—onstage—and for the people with whom I felt the most comfortable—strangers. Busying myself with America 88x50 allowed the rest of me to incubate in a way that I'd never really experienced before, and I started wondering why life outside the tour—for instance, life at home—should be any less honest. Restless to get back out there again, to keep growing again, to owe no persona to anyone again except that of the concert pianist—it was tough, sure, but easier to pull off than this life in the closet—I stewed in the passenger seat, remembering the time my mother, my loving, supportive, best friend of a mother, covered her eyes when the image of two men sharing a bed appeared on the television screen, and the time my stepfather said he'd disown a gay son.

PORTLAND, MAINE

Growing up, I saw my dad at least once a month. We would go on fishing trips to Hampton Beach on the New Hampshire coastline, or to a nearby lake in Vermont, buzzing around in a small, aluminum boat, driving there in his ancient Ford pickup truck with a plastic milk jug between us sloshing with his tobacco spit. Sometimes we'd drive past Montpelier and cast our lines off the crumbling boat launch at Wrightsville Dam Reservoir, and even in that sad lagoon with its orange, rusty water, he always managed to catch a bass. My little red-and-white bobber would tuck below the surface and I'd reel in a sunfish.

My parents divorced when I was two but they maintained a close, if undefined, relationship that accompanied me through my childhood. Even though my mom eventually dated other men, and even though when I visited my dad's apartment in New Hampshire I'd find bras and phone numbers hiding about, it took them both getting remarried to other people, which they both did at about the same time, for me to stop thinking they'd ever end up back together. I was ten. He and I kept going on fishing trips.

But lately we rarely talked. I saw him once a year, usually around Christmas, often meeting in the same McDonald's parking lot on the Vermont-New Hampshire border where he and my mother used to transfer me. The halfway point.

It's hard to say what happened. My excuse was that music got in the way—in high school I played in an orchestra that rehearsed every weekend—and my father's excuse, I suppose, was that he suddenly had his hands full with a new wife and a new son. So life got in the way. Or maybe we were just too similar. Our approach to love was lazy. We trusted it to prevail through prolonged silences and months apart. Perhaps it did, or perhaps it didn't. Either way, we wouldn't dare admit that we missed those fishing trips—we simply weren't the type—and neither of us would ever go as far as to say I love you. I don't think we ever had, but I'm not sure we ever needed to. We always had our own language, and it included silence.

He came up from New Hampshire to my concert in Maine at the Portland Conservatory, and waited until the last of that night's audience[149] left to approach me.

"Do you know how to get back to Manchester okay?" I asked.

"Yes. It's real easy," he said.

"Thanks again for coming. I'm so glad you got to see...this." I swirled my arm around my head. "What I've been doing."

"I'm proud of you," he said. "And your health is good?" He always asked about my health. I'd inherited my colitis from his side of the family, and I think he felt some guilt for that.

"Yes, Dad. I'm all good."

"...'cause that's all that matters." We hugged goodbye and he turned toward the door to leave, but seemed to remember something and turned around. "Remember, I created you." He pointed his finger at me, smirking. "Don't forget that."

"I know, Dad," I said.

MIDDLETOWN, CONNECTICUT

Katie, my ex-girlfriend from high school, attended the show with her boyfriend, Craig, who was then earning a degree in theology with the goal, I think, of becoming a minister. About ten other people from around Middletown joined them. The Buttonwood Tree, my venue, was something between a bookstore and a chic performance space. The piano, a rare and

---

149 http://dissonantstates.com/post/13111972361/mainefragment

dusty Miller baby grand, put up a mighty fight with its tight action, uneven tuning, and even a soft pedal that shifted the keyboard so far to the right that all the notes modulated up a half-step if I dared press it. But the piano's placement, in front of a wall-length window, allowed me to gaze out onto the glassy street, wet with winter rain, as I played.

The concert wrapped without calamity, and though I was exhausted from my wrestling match with the Miller, I was still energized enough from the performance to drive another three-and-a-half hours back to Vermont, even though Katie offered me accommodations in her and Craig's apartment. I loaded my car as they watched. In an instant, rain started pouring again. "Jesus Chriiiiiiiist!" I cried, and then regarded Craig with an apology.

Even though Katie and I had never spent all that much time out of school together, when we broke up, she cried. I didn't know how to do what we were supposed to be doing, and so absorbed was I in preparing my conservatory audition program that it hardly dawned on me that I had any responsibilities elsewhere. But there we were, breaking up at a table in a private study room in the back of our high school library, a room filled with long-forgotten LPs where I introduced myself to the history of Western music, and I felt powerless in the face of her pain, awful for hurting her and angry at myself for letting the whole thing happen in the first place. With a flurry of promises never to speak to me again, she left, and I was alone with Bach's *St. Matthew Passion* playing. I stood up, took it off the turntable, replaced it with Ravel's *Daphnis and Chloe,* and resumed writing poetry about a new friend I'd met named Calvin.

PAWTUCKET, RHODE ISLAND

They stopped clapping before I even finished my bow, and I marched to the back of the Pawtucket Public Library's[150] main atrium[151] in silence, almost in shame; this was the first time in forty-one states that an audience declined an encore. I kept walking down a flight of stairs to the office of the library's director. "I think they actually hated it," I said.

"I was there," he answered, "and they liked it well enough to nearly lynch that guy whose phone kept going off. We'll know by who shows up to the meet-and-greet dinner."

"Oh right," I sighed. I'd almost forgotten. "The dinner." With a lump in my throat, I followed him in his car across Pawtucket as a blizzard began showering the city. We arrived at a small Italian restaurant replete with blue-collar families, couples, and, seated at a long table, was my entire audience. "Here he is!" someone shouted and everyone cheered, with me front and center, feeling incredible, like I'd just graduated high school.

WATCHUNG, NEW JERSEY

The Watchung Arts Center had included America 88x50 in its regular Sunday series, so I was more confident than usual in the chance that I'd have a strong audience. Howard, its director, stressed that he would promote the concert and asked for

---

150 http://media.dissonantstates.com/i/PawtucketLibrary.jpg

151 http://media.dissonantstates.com/i/PianoAtrium.jpg

a plethora of materials. I was excited enough about the prospect of having a sizable audience that I invited Rachel, once-girlfriend of Ben in Madison and still a close friend of mine, to come up for the concert from Princeton where she was studying. But when I arrived at the Watchung Arts Center with less than an hour to go before start time, the doors were locked and the place, eerily empty. I called Howard. After three rings, he picked up, sounding surprised. "You're there? Good. I plan on regulating the piano soon, so it'll be nice having you around."

"So *when* were you thinking about doing that?" I asked, looking at my watch.

"Well, since you're around, whenever's good for you. I have the afternoon free."

Okay, something was wrong. "I'm looking at the poster, Howard, and it says the concert is today, the twenty-fifth, and that it starts at four, which is in forty-five minutes."

"Wait a minute, let me get a calendar out." There was a sound of paper shuffling. "Holy shit." And that's when I knew. My venue had actually forgotten about my concert. "I can't believe no one else is there, either," he murmured to himself in disbelief.

"Do you think we'll have an audience?" I asked. "Since there's not even a staff?"

"I honestly thought you *always* had five people at your shows," said Rachel, sitting next to me in the front row of chairs that Howard had frantically set up around the piano[152] when he arrived at the gallery. "Plus, it went great, and those four ladies sitting with me had the *best* time. I was just talking with them in the other room." Howard had provided a small reception. "One of them really wants you to—"

"—*to play something she recognizes*," I finished for her. "Yeah, I know. She asked me to do the same thing. But that's not what this project is about," I whined, "or what it's *supposed* to be about." I gestured toward the piano, the empty room. "Honestly, I don't know what any of this is about anymore."

"You're okay," Rachel said assuredly. "It's all in your head. The concert was amazing."

Just then, a woman's voice echoed through the gallery. "Have you thought of something yet?"

Rachel shifted uncomfortably in her seat.

"Are you his girlfriend?" the voice continued.

I shifted uncomfortably in *my* seat. Before Rachel could answer, the woman fired yet another question. "And why was no one here?"

"I don't know," I said.

"You played so ferociously I thought the piano might crack in half!"

"Maybe I do have something I can play," I said. "It might be the only thing in my repertoire right now that you'll recognize." I stood up, my metal chair screeching against the wooden floor, and sat at the piano. I played an improvisation on "The Star-Spangled Banner[153]," and the woman sang along with her hand on her heart.

---

152 http://media.dissonantstates.com/i/JerseyPiano.jpg

153 http://media.dissonantstates.com/a/NationalAnthemImprov.mp3

FRIENDSHIP VILLAGE, MICHIGAN

It was around New Year's, three months ago, when I'd confirmed a concert at Friendship Village, Kalamazoo's premiere retirement community. I had entertained the idea of playing retirement communities from the very conception of America 88x50, back when I thought I'd try executing the entire tour without planning a single show. Nursing homes, I figured, would accept last-minute concerts with the least suspicion, like a walk-in. But Friendship Village was no joke. It had a number of performing arts facilities, including a large concert hall where I'd perform, called the Kiva, with a Steinway concert grand, and this particular hall typically had performers booked for months in advance. So while Friendship Village may have been a last resort for me, hosting America 88x50 had been an act of compassion for them.

That was the good news. The bad news, I suppose, was that the administration demanded my concert run no longer than an hour and fifteen minutes. Lately it ran a healthy two hours, so I'd have to perform it with no intermission and no explanations to even have a chance of meeting their timeframe. Friendship Village also made it clear that, while the concert was open to the public, they would make no effort to promote it. I sent a number of worthless e-mails to Kalamazoo's leading newspapers and radio stations.

Friendship Village stood on a hill like a compound. It was late March and there was a frozen spring feeling in the air, a thin smell of dead grass and petrified dirt. I parked the Hyundai and found the closest entrance, the Health Center, hoping that those inside could tell me where to find my key, as Friendship Village was also providing my accommodations that night in a guest room. My first sight was of several frail women in wheelchairs and endless fluorescent lights. "Health Center" was quite the euphemism; I'd expected a spa, this was a hospital. A nurse at the front desk directed me to the main office where I would find my key, and on the way there I came across the Kiva. It was a large, banquet-style room, not the auditorium I had in mind. Inside, a choir of Friendship Village residents sang an arrangement of "Let There Be Peace on Earth."

I continued walking, passing through libraries and lounges, the cafeteria[154], and past countless apartment doors individually decorated by the community residents inside. One might have mistaken this place for a college dormitory; many of the doors were covered with anti-war bumper stickers.

I play the concert in an hour and twenty minutes, standing only at the halfway mark to grab a bottle of water by the piano bench, drinking it in one gulp. No intermission. No encore. "You did well tonight, kid," says one resident as the room clears. "Bigger crowd than movie night."

I woke up at seven-thirty the next morning to the sound of flowing water. The half-globe of frosted glass surrounding my ceiling light was filled to the brim with water like an aquarium, spilling over in a sloppy

154 http://dissonantstates.com/post/13369005497/michiganfragment

waterfall. The ceiling was leaking, but water also seeped from cracks in the walls, the light fixtures, and the cabinets. It couldn't be from the roof—I was on the bottom floor of a three-story building—so what was happening? I shook off sleep and stood up, water rising and bubbling around my toes from the saturated carpet, and threw on some clothes. Just outside my door was an old man huddled over a puzzle, finished but for one or two pieces, and coming toward me were two female housecleaners.

"Water is pouring from my ceiling and shooting out of the walls," I said. And in a moment, Friendship Village was aflutter with activity, employees running not only to my room but also up the flight of stairs next to it, calling for buckets, vacuums, assistance. I had a breakfast voucher, so I walked away and to the dining room, unnerved, convinced that someone had died in the room above me. There was no way someone could sleep through a flood like that, so intense that it began submerging *my* room below it. They would've been up to their neck in water. And I doubted that someone went on vacation in the middle of the night and forgot to turn off the faucet.

So what had I been doing when they expired? Desperately trying to establish a dial-up connection to the Internet on my laptop on a barely-long-enough phone cable pulled tight across the room like tripwire, to check my e-mail and, of course, peruse the local fare of similarly desperate men in Kalamazoo. I never established the connection, but had I, would I really have invited someone to Friendship Village? Probably not. Just like I wouldn't have really summoned anyone to the top of a mountain in Hawaii. No, for all my prowling, my single real-life tryst in America 88x50 had still only been Shane, who was certainly more than a hookup, who I needed to call back, who had just told me in a voicemail that he'd gotten the job at that juvenile facility he was interviewing for, and that it would probably take up a lot of his time, and that it would start very soon.

At breakfast, a female resident who attended the previous night's concert sat next to me. "I was hoping you'd be here so I could give this to you!" she said, slipping me a religious pamphlet. I thanked her, filed it in my pocket, and got straight to describing that morning's episode in my room. "Oh," she shivered, surveying the cafeteria. "Somebody probably just left the water running. It happens."

AUGUSTA AND CONYERS, GEORGIA

I zoomed by my third dead dog in three days, a yellow lab split in half, neon-red blood splashed across the interstate shoulder, an unwelcome sight amidst the expanding, silky Kentucky meadows. My car later soared and swiveled through the Smoky Mountains, clutching rigid walls of rock and pine suspended over meandering rivers below with their beautiful browns and reflections of gold dust in the spring air. The highway shot through tunnels, penetrating and defying even the most imposing mountainsides, my radio going dead and leaving me only with the sudden sound of containment, pressure, isolation.

When I arrived in Augusta, I could barely see straight, weary from eleven hours on the road and dizzied by the flickering bulbs of restaurant awnings and plantation-sized car dealerships that flanked the road leading to my host Cindy's house. She lived, however, in a quiet neighborhood ruled by the sound of cicadas, and appeared at her front door just as I stumbled toward it. A giant dog[155] joined her, looking like a brontosaurus and wearing a tiny pair of jean shorts around its hind end, a huge whip of a tail sticking out and waving through the air, slapping the wall with shuddering smacks. "Watch out for that tail, honey. It really stings," she said. "Oh, she's in heat. That's what the shorts are about."

"She wears it to attract the boys?" I asked in an exhausted attempt at humor.

"No, just the opposite. It's her chastity belt," Cindy answered, leading me inside. "I prepared you a plate. Sweet tea, broiled fish, and asparagus." I sneezed. "Bless you. Probably the pollen, honey." She handed me a plate. "Did you see downtown?"

"The car dealerships?" I asked, my mouth already full.

She laughed. "Okay, so you drove in a different way. Downtown is different. You'd like it there. It was totally dead a few years back when the box stores came to the outside of town—sucked it all right up—and people only came to Augusta for the Masters." She searched my face. "Golf? The annual Masters Golf Tournament?"

"Ah," I said, shrugging. "Wow."

"Well, if you were into golf you'd've already known about Augusta," she said. "But you know, it wasn't the Masters that saved this city. It was the *arts*, the people who set up little galleries in the empty storefronts. *They* started the rebirth that brought our downtown back. The arts saved Augusta from the malls!"

---

155 http://media.dissonantstates.com/i/DogShorts.jpg

"So is that where your organization has me playing?" I asked. "Downtown?"

"No, we have you at an elementary school. And it's not really in a great area." She scrunched her nose. "Not downtown."

It didn't seem like *such* a bad area. If anything, quiet. The brick houses seemed maybe a little dirty, but that seemed about it. But then, what did I know?

In the school auditorium, sunlit by large windows on the sidewalls, a rented Yamaha baby grand already stood on the stage glimmering like a glassy black sculpture. Three hundred and fifty students, kindergarten through fifth grade, sat row by wooden row in restless awe of the foreign instrument, this alien object on the stage. Mine would be the first piano recital in the school's history. The principal, dressed in bright pink, took the microphone.

"Hello, everybody!" she began. "This young man beside me is a famous pianist." My eyes widened. I almost laughed. "He's traveling all fifty states to play concerts for schools just like ours. He even just played in a *nursing home!*" I suppressed a cringe, scanning the perimeter of the room where staff members stood, afraid that they, especially any music teachers, would be skeptical of a "famous pianist" who played elementary schools and nursing homes.

But the crowd was nothing but supportive, and after my demonstration several children asked for autographs, coming at me with sticky-notes and shreds of paper to sign. One girl asked me to sign her hand.

"What's your name?" I asked.

"Quintáshia."

A middle-aged woman in faded clothes thanked me for bringing America 88x50 to this corner of Augusta. "No one else would come here," she said emphatically, and put some crinkled money into the hat beside my CDs, taking one and walking off to reveal a small boy in overalls, waiting behind her with his hand outstretched.

"I just wanted to say yer doin' a real good job," he said in a high voice and heavy Southern drawl.

"Thanks, buddy." I shook his hand. "Do you play?"

"Naw. Used to, but we moved and had to sell the piano."

"Was it like that one there?" I asked, pointing to an upright in the corner.

"No, it was like the one up there." He pointed to the Yamaha.

"Do you like it here in Augusta?" I didn't know what else to ask.

He nodded his head, glowing, and then gestured with his chin toward the woman who had just bought a CD. "Yeah. Me and my mom live just down the street."

I had two concerts in Georgia, the next one a few days later in Conyers, a town just east of Atlanta. With about a half-hour till showtime, the vice president of my presenting organization discovered that she had only brought keys to the front door of the venue and had forgotten the keys to the actual hall. We could only get partially inside. "The woman who normally does this is out of town!" she explained, blustering out the door onto the street. I knew that. I was staying with that woman's family.

Fifteen minutes later, when the vice president returned with a key that accessed the hall, but not the tech booth or even the bathroom, I also realized that we had no programs. "In a town like Conyers," she said, "I don't think people really need programs."

"I play over twenty pieces in this recital," I said. "We need programs." I dug into my bag and handed her one of my generic program pages. "Make copies." At this point, there were already nearly two-dozen people in the hall, and they watched as she again stomped out. Backstage, I found a dirty sink and washed my hands in its cold water with a fossilized bar of soap. I started the concert without programs and in two hours was already gone, in and out of this town like a faint, inconsequential memory.

PART THREE

MOBILE, ALABAMA

After he kills you, everyone will know. They'll know it was never about the piano, never about your country, never about finding yourself, but rather about burying yourself. Dancing deeper and deeper into the closet until you become unrecognizable and indistinguishable from the closet itself. And this is that moment, the moment you realize the tour was never anything but a means to an end, and this is that end, a Motel 6 in Mobile, Alabama, at two in the morning.

I tear across the room and whip the shades closed. Hands shaking, I chain the door and turn off the lights. I trip over a stack of tattered scores and send them cascading across the carpet, which reminds me to shove these scores, practice keyboard too, all under the bed. I don't want him knowing what I do. If he comes. If I let him in. And what if I don't? What will he do? Will he tap the window? Will he shout for me to open the door and wake up the rest of the motel? Will he find my car—I typed to him that I was from Vermont—and smash its windows? Take the money? Everyone will know.

I jump into bed and clutch the covers over my head as if a poltergeist is circling the room. What would they think, tomorrow's audience for my concert and master class, if they could see me now, here under the covers, breathless and terrified? Well, it doesn't matter, because soon they'll know. Everyone will know.

No. I grab my laptop and unlock the series of bolts on the door, swinging it open and running to my little blue Hyundai as if I'm being chased through the parking lot by a tornado. I smell the burning rubber as I drive to another motel parking lot a quarter mile down the interstate's feeder road. I'll find another wireless signal, I tell myself, and he'll appear online again, and he'll say he never left his house, that he chickened out, and I'll say, *Oh, that's cool I'm heading to bed anyway* and I'll return to my room, vowing never to do this again, and I'll play my concert tomorrow with a lesson learned. Just a little tired.

But there's no wireless signal. I can't get online. So I drive back. I park. I close the door to my room, and I stand there. Maybe he came while I was gone.

And then I hear a series of hollow knocks. I jump, my heart pumps acid from my chest to the seat of my pelvis, freezing my veins and spreading across my stomach and thighs like a virus. I creep to the door and peek through the keyhole. He appears maybe ten years older than me, with tan skin and dark hair. He has a muscular build, handsome, and when I finally open the door, he stands silently before me, allowing me to scan his body. His clothes are loose and dusty, and when I motion him in, he walks past me with the sheepish gait of a child who's been called to the principal's office. He sits at the synthetic table by the struggling air conditioner and I sit opposite him on the bed.

We politely acquaint ourselves for almost an hour, warming up, talking casually, as if it's just by chance that he wandered into my motel room at half-past two in the morning. A nervous energy underlies each sentence, and we veil our conversation with a safety net of half-truths and reserved details so as not to reveal too much about our lives, the people we love, and the things we cherish in the light of day. We're co-conspirators and co-inhabitants of the same closet world, where identities and dreams are equally shrouded and shameful and impossibly remote. But I do know he works construction, races cars, and has a wife and step-kids. He knows I'm on a fifty-state tour and that I play the piano.

The television blares the Home Shopping Network. A woman is selling knives.

"I don't want to force anything on you," I say finally. "We can just talk, like we said on the computer. I mean… this is all kind of weird for—"

"It is for me, too." He begins to squirm in his seat and purrs with an Alabama drawl, "I'm bashful."

"Well, you can come over here." I pat the bed.

Now we're side by side at the edge of the mattress like it's a bench, back at the principal's office, and I put a hand on his shoulder and the other arm across his chest, lightly gripping the muscle there. I forget that I was ever scared and pull his shirt off.

His face comes inches from mine. He pins me to the bed, our legs tangled. He holds my chest down with a calloused hand and puts the other between my legs. I wrestle him under me and begin to slowly taste the sweat collecting in the small of his back with little butterfly kisses. I move down, down, down his body until I find his leg, worshipping his left thigh and running my tongue along a scar that runs deep across it. The skin around the wound is soft and purple and wrinkled and tastes tart and foreign, like lips.

He grabs both my shoulders and pulls me up. We consume mouth, tongue, armpit, nipple, muscle, hair, ear, neck, beards, as our strong arms rub and pull each other closer, harder, hysterically grinding like an engine into a high-geared, breathless sobbing, a rapture, like we need to absorb each other completely to temporarily diffuse, as only we can do for each other, the shared, secret need that brought us here.

He flips me over and shoves my face into the starched motel sheets.

This wasn't the plan.

Yes, it hits me in a cold wave of clarity. This is my first time receiving, submitting. Bottoming. This construction worker, this stepfather of three, this stranger, will be my first, and never from this moment on will I be able to fully distance myself from this motel room, this gutted coastal city, this man, this act. Him. Me. It. This tour. We're all inseparable. Starting now.

I gasp. I clench. His hips pump faster. My body screams, my voice chokes and sputters. He doesn't stop. And after a few agonizing minutes, it starts to change, this feeling, and I feel myself changing too, and I know that I'm not going to ask him to stop or make him stop or even let him stop. Not until he's done. The palm of his hand grips my shoulder, then runs down my braced arm. His fingers, fat and thick and petrified with dust and labor, weave through the fingers of my pianist hand.

He turns me on my back, and I glance from his scruffy face, his eager, enraged, ashamed eyes to my legs in the air, and now I'm ashamed too, so I look to the television screen and see a knife cutting through a mound of raw meat with little blood bubbles collecting on the cutting board. I close my eyes. He thrusts harder. Faster. I feel used, but useful. And it doesn't hurt. Not anymore.

I want to collect every nuance—hear him, see him—so I open my eyes and bring my gaze to his. His eyes dart and blink and roll in a manic short-circuit of ecstasy and defeat. His neck tenses. I can see his pulse through a long, thick vein running up from his shoulder. Out of breath, he collapses, slips out and away from me, and stands at the edge of the bed, snapping off the condom he brought. It looks heavy, and I feel proud looking at it. I'm responsible for that, I tell myself. He disappears into the bathroom and turns on the faucet. I myself didn't finish, but I still feel completed somehow. When he appears a minute later and sits beside me on the bed, our backs against the headboard, I reach my arm around him and stroke the back of his head. He squirms, and I can tell he doesn't want this anymore. I stop.

"So how many states have you hit?" he asks, his voice deeper than before, reset, like we're making small talk at a hardware store.

"Alabama will be forty-five."

He nods in approval. "Where will it end?"

I'm not sure what to say, and repeat his question with a sigh. "Where will it end... Well, after Arizona I'll leave my car in L.A., fly home to Vermont, play the final concert, then I'll..." I pause, staring at his leg again. "How'd you get that scar?"

His tired eyes drag to mine, and a little grin smears across his face. "A chainsaw."

The Alabama concert went almost embarrassingly well. The master class[156] was a total success, and the full audience in the Eastern Shore Arts Center crowded the gallery and heaped on their applause when my recital ended. For once, I didn't suspect anything of it. I actually agreed with them. At state forty-five, I'd hit my stride. Between pieces I worked the floor like a comedian and in performance I commandeered the piano like—well, a pianist.

I signed an autograph for someone who told me, "The last time I asked for a pianist's autograph was almost thirty years ago, and it was Van Cliburn." Another said, "This was the best concert I've seen here, and I've sponsored them since 1987." A couple gray-haired foxes showered me with compliments. One said I was "graceful," the other, "sexy." I left with two hundred and sixty-five dollars cash and promises of checks in the mail.

---

156 http://media.dissonantstates.com/i/AlabamaMasterclass.jpg

The road is an unflinching psychiatrist. It doesn't speak, just listens. From the backwoods emptiness of Alabama's Highway 231 where I passed a Baptist church marquee[157] that read: PUSH: PRAY UNTIL SOMETHING HAPPENS, to Florida's 98 West along the Gulf where a hurricane-damaged neon sign[158] read: WELCO E TO PENSEC L BEA H!, to busy Interstate 10 into Mobile and now, onward into Biloxi, I had some time to think. I thought a little about my father, the fishing trips we went on, the nights we watched boxing matches on his hotwired cable box, the days I'd observe him grilling steaks and fixing cars. All this coupled with his long absences and the mystery of when he'd return and how long he'd stay.

My house was an almost totally feminine environment, with a single mother working two jobs—she was a teacher and a hostess—and two gorgeous older sisters. As much as his off-and-on presence brightened my world, my dad's influence on the household was ephemeral and sporadic at best. Any fear of being *different* as a kid I probably owed less to his prejudices (if he had any) and more to the general mid-eighties teenage culture of my sisters, for which I had a front row seat. In that world, the word "gay" meant lame, and it was used to near exhaustion. I used it, too, even after I knew it had another meaning, a meaning I could already feel growing and gaining power inside me, like I was pregnant with that feeling.

Was I born with it? I didn't know. The women in my life were divine, heroic, untouchable. Family. And perhaps subsequently, I grew up with a kind of holy reverence, and thus aversion, to the female body. It was

---

157 http://media.dissonantstates.com/i/Marquee.jpg
158 http://media.dissonantstates.com/i/PensacolaSign.jpg

sacred. I'll never forget discovering an adult magazine in the woods as a kid and recoiling. Looking at the female anatomy splayed out like that seemed like some kind of gross betrayal to the domestic femininity I knew and understood. Eventually, shock became indifference. By the time my oldest sister moved away and started appearing in racy, albeit never pornographic, magazines herself (which made me something of a sixth grade celebrity) I didn't give it a second thought. Leafing through Playboy unfazed, it was just cool to have a famous sister.

Driving west on Interstate 10, I knew this all sounded like oversimplified drugstore psychology, but even if I was rationalizing, for once I wasn't despairing. For once there was no anger, guilt, or confusion, and with every mile my mind clawed its way closer to some semblance of an explanation, an answer as to why I was the way I was, and any answer would do. Today it might be nurture, tomorrow it could be nature, but at least there was an *it*, finally an *it*, when a year ago there had only been denial and rationalizations of another kind. A year ago I had a problem, an addiction, some kind of tick that maybe I could push through or pass like a bladder stone. Nature versus nurture? As if I cared. And what if it was both? With Biloxi twenty-something miles away, I sank into my earliest, foggiest memories of secret tumbles with boys in the neighborhood, romps that would begin before I knew what sexuality was and that would continue long after when I knew to keep mine a secret. One of these times, when I was six or seven, my mom caught me under the bed in a sixty-nine position with a boy from my first grade class. I begged her only for one thing. Not to tell my sisters.

BILOXI, MISSISSIPPI

Online, I found a volunteer camp in Biloxi called Hands On, full of ambitious college students, hippies, misfits, hitchhikers, road people, and capitalists like myself who didn't mind the imposition of long days under the Mississippi sun dismantling the houses of the dead and displaced as long as it meant free food and shelter. This would be my home for the week as I waited for my Biloxi concert.

I rolled into the Hands On compound in my sporty Hyundai, cell phone in hand, wearing sunglasses and a white T-shirt and jeans, introducing myself to the main administrators—I'd e-mailed them earlier—and staking out a little nook in the sleeping area, a loft lined with cots, sleeping bags, and even tents, winding around the perimeter of what was usually a large warehouse. In the middle, one could look down to the ground floor where there were dozens of tables set up for meals.

The colorful personalities of my fellow volunteers intimidated me immediately. My tales of America 88x50, the fact I was even *doing* it, seemed unimpressive in the face of their personal histories, their own extensive travels. Entering Hands On was like entering a web of complex inside jokes, hierarchies, and communities, all the way down to who slept inside and who braved the outdoors[159]. Some of them had been here for six months, some since the storm itself. I overheard someone, an older man, say that Hands On reminded him of the communes he frequented during the sixties. "It's a life where everything is free," he said, "and all you do is drink and have sex and help people."

---

159 http://media.dissonantstates.com/i/HandsOnCamp.jpg

On my first night, I tagged along with nearly twenty people from Hands On for a pilgrimage to Just Us, a gay bar in Biloxi. None of them seemed to be gay, so I figured that Just Us was more or less a regular hangout for the volunteers and, for all I knew, may have been one of the only surviving bars in Biloxi. I didn't ask. I didn't care. I just went.

And I drank, heavily, determined to fit in, determined to penetrate that intimidating Hands On society and seal my popularity for the rest of my time there, which was only practical. After all, I needed to ensure an audience for my concert later that week in a church on Highway 90 right across from the water, its pews cleared out by Katrina. The piano survived. A miracle, they called it.

It was karaoke night at Just Us, and I had a flash of inspiration. I would do karaoke! Something over the top. I'd never done karaoke before, but this could be some great PR for the concert, and no longer would I be that new kid who sulked around camp earlier in the day. I would be the performer, the life of the party, brave and brazen and without a shred of self-consciousness. Pencil in hand, I wrote "Kiss—Prince" on a pad.

When I heard my name, the world seemed to go into slow motion. I climbed the stage, feeling my body move but my brain stuck somewhere else, perhaps back at the bar, my reasoning self watching me with just as bemused and unfamiliar a gaze as everyone else, doing its best to keep my fear and doubt and what-the-hell-are-you-doing far, far away. The music came on and I felt my mouth open, hearing my falsetto zing through the speakers and across the room like it was someone else's.

But it *was* me, in a Biloxi gay bar, with a bunch of strangers, singing Prince. And I was doing pretty damn well. Yes, all the way down to the final screams of the song, all the way down to the backup dancers I'd recruited at the last minute. I was functioning out of body, out of mind, and it felt familiar, like one of the rare but perfect moments at the piano when my music, mind, and body all aligned. In a way, I *had* done this before.

Someone handed me a free drink and I went outside to get some air, dripping with sweat. "Was that you?" asked a short, muscular man with a beard and a tight, high voice. I nodded. "Sounded just like the CD," he said, and then approached. "So you one of them do-gooders? Coming here, working for free and stealing the work right out of Biloxi?"

"I'm just passing through," I answered.

"Bunch of do-gooders coming down here for extra credit, think you're helping with your projects and your reports to your college professors and church groups. Girls doing construction in their tube tops, looking down on all of us like we're victims. I was in the *Army!* Special forc—"

"Listen," I interrupted. "I just needed a place to stay. I'm not a do-gooder."

"That so?"

"Yeah, that's right."

While working in the houses of the dead and displaced, we met those neighbors who survived, and furthermore, who chose to stay, living in campers and

FEMA trailers, and often they would come out and tell us their stories—stories about bodies in the streets and people drowned in attics. One day they decided to prepare us a crawfish boil as a gesture of gratitude.

So with Massenet's opera *Manon* playing on the public radio station, crackling from a small portable radio, we volunteers took a break from mold removal and ate crawfish in our bodysuits, listening less to the Massenet and more to the family. They didn't call Katrina a storm. They called it a flood, explaining that a giant wave swept north from the Gulf over the little finger of land on which Biloxi sits, demolishing nearly everything and everyone in its path, and emptying into the bay directly north of that little finger of land. But like any wave, big or small, it had to return to sea. "So we got it twice," said our cook, stirring the crawfish pot, his face dripping with sweat as he smiled and shook his head in disbelief.

"I tell you," added his wife. "I can still see the places that aren't here anymore. I pass by the spot where an old friend's house was, but I still see it. I still see their house. I still see them."

Even eight months after the storm—the *flood*, I mean—the city was still in ruins, looking like the aftermath of a nuclear holocaust[160], much worse than what I saw in Mobile a few days earlier. All industry that once occupied the beachfront had been claimed by the sea, with nothing but bare-bones parking lots remaining on its twisted metal banks, demolished signs still standing

---

160 http://media.dissonantstates.com/i/BiloxiCollapse.jpg

guard over the empty foundations of fast-food chains. A ravaged Waffle House[161]. The ghost of a Taco Bell[162]. Cemeteries were overturned[163], headstones cracked in half, tombs collapsed and opened[164].

Highway 90 had once been a shady, tree-lined boulevard of mansions on the seashore. Now only a few trees survived, their skeletal limbs raped and mangled, some trunks completely ripped from the ground and displaced upon roofs, folding the houses inward[165], so vulgar it was almost funny. The houses that remained were barely standing, many torn open and exposing to passersby like myself a glimpse inside[166] at the life that once was—a decaying corpse of a living room that still retained its carpeted staircase leading to what might have once been a bedroom. This was the end of the world. One house bore a message scrawled[167] in white spray paint: WE ARE HOME!! WILL SHOOT NO LOOTING!

"Three in the front row," Sister Mary whispered to me, not moving her mouth, as a small class of first and second graders filed into the classroom. "Four there in the second row. Four in the third. And all but one in the back row. All three teachers standing in the back of the room,

161 http://media.dissonantstates.com/i/BiloxiWaffleHouse.jpg

162 http://media.dissonantstates.com/i/BiloxiTacoBell.jpg

163 http://media.dissonantstates.com/i/BiloxiCemetery.jpg

164 http://media.dissonantstates.com/i/BiloxiTombs.jpg

165 http://media.dissonantstates.com/i/BiloxiHouse.jpg

166 http://media.dissonantstates.com/i/BiloxiHouseInside.jpg

167 http://media.dissonantstates.com/i/BiloxiWillShoot.jpg

too. Lost everything. I mean, *everything*. In the morning, there are pillows and sleeping bags lining the hallways here. These are middle- and upper-class families, sleeping on the floor of a Catholic elementary school."

The room fell silent as the children waited for Sister Mary to reveal whom I was and why I'd come to their school. She shifted to a cheerier tone, turning from me to the group. "Mr. Adam is here from Vermont, and has spent the whole year traveling all fifty states to play the piano…"

I played "The Night Winds" by Griffes, something I usually played for kids because it was fast and evocative, but here it felt different, and indeed the reaction was different, starting with the first student who shouted, "It sounds like Katrina!" And so began a crossfire of stories from children who had been at the frontlines of a hurricane, all outshouting each other, each story more fantastically surreal than the next, and of course I had no doubt all of them were true. Sister Mary had no visible reaction. Surely she'd heard these stories before.

Afterward, the room was jammed with students leaving, and a little girl close to me seemed trapped and upset by the commotion. I crouched down and whispered to her, "You know, my mom's a teacher and she doesn't like it either when polite girls like you have to wait for other kids to calm down. It isn't fair, is it?"

She looked at me, the two pink ties in her hair a perfect foil to the two dark circles under her eyes. "Life isn't fair," she answered plainly, automatically, as if she'd heard those words many times before and was just repeating them.

☆

The camp voted to eat dinner early the night of my concert because the times conflicted, and my fellow volunteers, many of whom over the course of the week I'd grown close to—some of us went to a county fair the night before—slowly filled up the metal chairs circling the piano. I watched from the choir loft, where a man was setting up a video camera. "I'll take some footage of the road outside, too," he told me. "So you remember what it looked like."

When I played, I didn't think or analyze. I let my body channel the music in its perfection, its brutal energy[168], feeding off the human electricity there in that circle, a feeling of solidarity, a warped patriotism we all seemed to share—I silenced the intermission with my improvisation on "The Star-Spangled Banner"[169] to bring people back to their seats—the same kind of warped patriotism I discovered emanating from the program since the fall, a patriotism that actually made room for the tragedies of our government, the tragedies of our history, the tragedies of what happened here in Biloxi, because this American music I played in America 88x50 made room for such tragedy. I hit practically every note—or at least so it seemed—even if my hands were still swollen from days of tearing out the floorboards of destroyed homes, places where people had died.

When the concert finished, and after a reception on the front lawn where a humid Gulf breeze blew, I re-entered the church and played for another hour, ironing out passages I thought needed improvement—*still* could use improvement—and then improvising softly

168 http://www.youtube.com/watch?v=uhuifugLk_4
169 http://www.youtube.com/watch?v=i2txFXVGnSc

and slowly as the remaining church staff, many of them volunteers from across the country themselves, boarded up the front doors with large sheets of wood. "Saw you on the TV[170] yesterday," one of them said as we all left. "I'm glad you played here."

Part of me suspected, maybe hoped, that the night would end at Just Us, but instead I returned to Hands On, showering in an outside stall under the stars, swigging a bottle of beer as the hot water ran across my aching muscles, and then I went inside, where most of the volunteers were already asleep in the balcony above. I ate some leftovers, wincing each time I swallowed, my throat stinging and swollen from all the dust and mold I'd breathed in that week, and some other volunteers straggled in and sat across from me. We began to whisper and I learned that two of them, a husband and wife, not only had come to the concert that evening, but had also lived in Vermont until just recently. "We sold everything," said the wife. "We wanted to live in the moment and go on the road."

"It's funny how," I tried to swallow a mouthful of rice, "people here lost everything and *had* to start over, but you both just *decided* to start over."

"Our kids are gone," she replied matter-of-factly, keeping her voice quiet, her sun-bleached hair glowing, her mouth always smiling, "and we wanted to see the country, to live in different places, experience new things, find ourselves in situations we never could have imagined, like your concert tonight. We never would have gone to something like that in Vermont, but we did tonight because it was here, and *we* were here, and you were here!"

---

170 http://www.youtube.com/watch?v=Sc4Bx6TbLB4

"Of course, it's not easy," whispered her husband, nodding to the balcony. "But it's possible. And because living this way is possible, it somehow seems...I don't know...right now it just seems..."

"Necessary," we all said at once.

NEW ORLEANS, LOUISIANA

A black cloud surrounds St. Bernard Parish. Street lights swing like relics, not working—there still isn't any electricity—and fast-food chains and box stores remain as mere water-logged souvenirs of the past, their windows either shattered or boarded, their veneers tagged by spray paint. Rooftops float through swamps, and boats in various states of demise sit boldly in the median of the highway. Debris is piled several stories high in the parking lots, though most garbage seems to be blowing through the streets.

I wake up on a cot, streams of sunlight shooting through holes in the ceiling of a large army tent[171] in a volunteer camp called Emergency Communities[172]. My eyes are crusted over with gunk, nearly sealed shut, and I feel waxy fluid flowing out of their corners down my cheeks. I sit up with a start, cough, and break my eyelids open with my fingers. Throwing off a thatch blanket and standing up, I stretch and stumble through the inside of the tent[173] and, once outside, run directly to a porta-potty, my insides twitching violently, my stomach

---

171 http://media.dissonantstates.com/i/ArmyTent.jpg

172 http://dissonantstates.com/post/13683617167/louisianafragment

173 http://media.dissonantstates.com/i/ArmyTentInside.jpg

screaming. Once inside the stall, I catch my reflection in a small stained mirror on the backside of the door. My face has red spots all over it, like flea bites, and I have a giant, unexplainable black welt under my left eye. I hover over the latrine and feel my colon explode, emptying endlessly, splashing into the blue pool of water several feet below, and on the toilet paper, after cleaning myself, there it is, finally. Blood.

I'm thinking only two things: I'm due to stay here another night, and I'm expected to play a mini-recital for a room full of schoolchildren downtown in two hours. I don't know how I'm going to do either.

Maryse was the wife of an eminent New Orleans composer, and together they would host my concert out of the church where he played organ. She had a high, tinny voice with a heavy French accent, often intermingling French with her English. She probably weighed seventy pounds soaking wet, and was so frail that she shook when she stood still or braced to take a photo, which was the first thing she did when I met her at the church. I tried hiding my face. "Oh, and after you called from the car, I found a place for you to stay tonight!" she said. "No more St. Bernard Parish. You will stay with our friends in a beautiful house[174] right here in the Garden District!" I nearly fainted with relief. "Also, do you sing?" I nodded. I'd say yes to anything at this point. Sing, dance, whatever she wanted. "Great!" she said, clapping her hands. "We need tenors for Sunday's

---

174 http://media.dissonantstates.com/i/GardenDistrictDigs.jpg

Easter[175] service. Rehearsal is tonight. Let's get you a robe. Your little concert for the kids is in twenty minutes, but come, we have time!"

"Life is a series of deaths and resurrections[176]," says the minister on Easter morning. "We fail and we die. We start over and we are reborn. Over and over. And this is life." Between the service and my five o'clock concert, I search the city for a pharmacy that carries the specific cortisone enemas I think will help me out of my flare-up. I've become something of an expert on ulcerative colitis over the past couple years, and am filling this prescription without consulting my doctors, my family, anybody. I don't want to create a panic—I'm panicking enough already. I look like death[177]. It can't be hard for anyone to see that something's wrong.

The Rite Aid carrying my enemas functions out of a small trailer.

Driving through the city, I keep looking to the Superdome. It's like a celebrity to me, and when I see the large gash of paneling still missing from the roof, I'm brought back to all the images from the news, back to September in Vermont when my mother and I brought bags of clothes to a drop-off center in Montpelier. Back when my sister was getting married. Back when I first started talking to Shane.

175 http://dissonantstates.com/post/13862506101/
neworleansfragment

176 http://dissonantstates.com/post/497440783/resurrection

177 http://media.dissonantstates.com/i/AdamDeath.jpg

The last time he and I talked was in Mobile. A six-pack of microbrews gifted to me in Georgia had exploded in my trunk during the afternoon heat while I volunteered at a data-entry center for the Red Cross (something I incorrectly assumed would earn me some free housing; I ended up staying instead at the Motel 6). And while scrubbing the coagulated beer off the seats and windows at a busy drive-thru carwash, I'd called Shane, hoping he would answer because lately he didn't pick up when I called, probably busy with his new job. He answered, but seemed only half-there, and he didn't even think my story about an entire six-pack of beer exploding in my car was funny. Probably tired, I thought. I told him I thought that glass bottles only exploded in the cold, not in the heat. He said, "They explode in both, buddy."

A woman compliments my performance, adding that the man she came with, sitting in a wheelchair a few pews back from the piano, also enjoyed it. I follow her finger. "Him?" I ask. "Really? I was watching him, and he had his hands covering his ears the whole time!"

"Oh, no!" she laughs. "He was just holding his head up so he wouldn't fall asleep."

I'm just about to leave the church when a stocky boy with a buzzed haircut—it looks like he did it himself— comes up to me and says, "You're like, living my dream."

"Well, if I can do this, anyone can," I say, bending down to arrange my small duffel bag. "I can't promise you'll find what you're looking for, but…"

"You did," he says.

"Excuse me?"

"Found what you came out here for. The way you play and talk and live *for* music. You found your passion. I see it. And there's no way you can come away from a tour like this and not understand what it means to be an artist in America."

"Really?" I crouch again to zip up my bag. "That's interesting. I have no idea."

"I think you're just saying that," he says. I stand up straight. "I've been reading about this part of our brain called the *accumbens* something or other that releases endorphins as well as dopamine, and these chemicals make you feel happy. In fact, they make you feel a lot more than that. They give you feelings of contentment. For a thinker like you, it's probably new information that really gives you a thrill. Understanding. Understanding is the most beautiful of all information. It's the most truthful. If you want to look at it in a domineering way, it's power. Your power."

I laughed and shook my head.

"You can laugh it off, but *I* think you found it. I was in the audience. I saw it. It's probably just easier for you to think that nothing's happened out here because then you can keep searching and never have to admit that you found what you were looking for, that you were successful. Admitting you did what you set out to do would mean you'd have to move on."

I don't say anything.

"Sorry if I'm being blunt," he says. "I just feel like I have a responsibility to be honest with you."

"Why?" My legs are shaking as if they might run off without me. "Why are you so interested?"

"Because you inspired me." He cocks his eyebrows. "You're a very talented guy. I've never gotten a reaction like that out of a crowd. They stood, they shouted."

"They plugged their ears."

"I, too, want to take a journey like yours, and it's truth and understanding that I also seek." He pauses. "I also seek fame, which I guess is a kind of power."

HOUSTON, TEXAS

I spotted a motel off the side of Interstate 45 just south of the hazy, impressive Houston skyline. It was thirty-five dollars a night and there was a Chinese food restaurant in the lounge. Perfect. My room was a retro explosion of shag carpet and dim lights, the switches for which were on the headboard of my king-size bed. From a swivel chair, I turned on the television to discover several channels of free pornography. I sat before the set, fixated. And across the interstate was an adult video store and theater, its parking lot filled always to capacity with trucks. I'd heard about those kinds of places and the things that happen inside. With my health getting back on track and my silent piano ignored on the bed, I sat alone with the adult movie channel and my chat rooms for a day, a night, and into the next morning, doing nothing but watching, chatting, and edging, until it was finally time to get dressed and visit Houston Public Radio for a live interview and performance[178].

---

178 http://media.dissonantstates.com/a/KUHFCompleteBroadcast.mp3

Multicultural Education and Counseling through the Arts, MECA for short, took over a converted public school building in Houston's Sixth Ward, the one neighborhood in Houston without a single new home or condo built in it. Once a uniformly poor and dangerous neighborhood, the Sixth Ward was now vigilant about retaining its historical integrity in the face of Houston's no-zoning construction craze. This is what I was told by MECA's executive director, Alice, matron of the Houston Chicano community. She took me out of my retro motel digs on I-45 and put me up in a Best Western at the foot of downtown, regularly dropping in to pick me up and take me to lunch, to dinner, and for tours of the city, which is a lot to say for a woman whose phone never stopped ringing with calls about protests, calls about problem students, calls about families facing threats of deportation.

Playing in MECA's official theater, converted from a cafeteria—a sign actually read CAFETORIUM—all the notes fell into place. I played with vigor and concentration. A photo[179] taken during this performance shows my body buried in the keyboard with both elbows up by my ears in ninety-degree angles, like a bird of prey. A board member of a local new music presenter attended, and after the recital he casually floated the idea of me returning to Houston after America 88x50 to serve as their organization's new artistic director.

Could I ever live in Houston? It was a hot, sprawling, concrete organism of a city, and the idea that I might someday call myself a Texan seemed so insanely remote

179 http://media.dissonantstates.com/i/MECAperformance.JPG

that I couldn't help but entertain it. I took his card.
Maybe I'd move to Texas[180].

One in the morning and back at the Best Western,
and I could feel it gnawing just behind my belly button,
itching along my hips and side. I wanted to see inside
that theater. This was it, my last night in Houston and
the tail end of the tour, and it would be as easy as taking
I-45 south and taking the same exit as that cheap motel
I stayed in with the Chinese restaurant and free porn.
Fifteen minutes, tops.

I was there in ten. The front parking lot was filled,
as usual, with pickup trucks, so I parked behind the
building. Entering through the back door, I squinted
underneath the white florescent lights and meandered
through rows of DVDs to an attendant elevated behind
a window at the front desk. I paid him five dollars and
walked through a hanging black curtain. Past the curtain,
the cement floor was immediately sticky and I couldn't
see anything. It was like a haunted house at Halloween,
people lurking in the darkness, hands touching, eyes
glowing. I could barely see, and walked either with my
hands outstretched like a zombie or feeling my way
along the wall. All the men seemed to be walking in circles around this cavernous maze, and I passed many of
them several times. Each time their eyes seemed more
and more insistent and expectant. Were mine, too?

There was a long hallway with tiny black doors on
each side, and inside each door was a small stall with a

---

180 http://dissonantstates.com/post/13925127464/texasfragments

television screen and channel changer below it. I walked down the hall and peered inside the open doors—men in various states of undress, not watching the smudged and smeared screen, but instead staring out at anyone who passed by. The doors that were closed had wide, round holes in them where the doorknobs should have been, but I didn't bend over to see what was happening inside; I could hear it and imagine the rest. At the end of the labyrinth was a larger movie theater with a screen in the front, rows of seats before it, and a couch in the back. There were men scattered about the room and a few on the couch, everyone watching each other, not the film, which I didn't really see either, everyone waiting for something to happen.

I repeated this circuit for about forty minutes before a smooth and young Mexican man whom I'd passed at least a dozen times met my eyes. He hadn't particularly interested me, and he still didn't, really, but after all this time invested, I let him pull me by the hand into one of the small booths. Inside—and he must have known this already—there was another man, older than both of us, with a thick gray moustache, wide hat, and droopy eyes like a basset hound, smoking a cigarette.

The young man dropped to his knees and alternated between the two of us. I felt the older man's hand against my chest and his eyes on me. My mind was screaming to leave—this didn't feel right—but I couldn't move. I just stared down at the young man, working diligently, wondering if this was a routine for him, or furthermore, for the older man standing with me. Faster and faster the boy worked until I finished with his mouth sealed around me, nothing escaping. There was a sound of him swallowing, and the sound of me beating the black wooden door with my clenched fist. And then, as he looked up and smiled, a familiar weight of clarity and guilt, something I'd never felt with Shane and something I thought might have been a thing of the past. The man on his knees returned his focus to the older guy in the hat, still smoking the same cigarette, and I stumbled backward out of the stall, backing up until I hit a closed door behind me.

I turned and, once more, started guiding myself through the darkness with my hand dragging along the wall until I felt a tugging, like my thumb was snagged on something, maybe a nail. I yanked and felt the flesh tear open, and blood began running down my hand. I started running, too, as if fueled by the awful thought of how every time I'd touch a piano from now until the end of the tour I'd be reminded of tonight, what I'd done, what I'd gone back to. I kept running into the white florescent lights of the video store, through the aisles and out the back door without ever looking back.

TUCSON, ARIZONA

Dear Adam,

I just keep reeling with delight at the thought of your performance yesterday, which I was lucky enough to attend—and I realized that part of what you have done is to take the ego out of it all—your humbleness and generosity in bringing such incredible music to us. You are a true artist for pursuing your passion and manifesting your talent without regard to shallow ambition. There are so many ways that this kind of spirit has impact—so many levels of inspiration reeling out from each performance—you are the kind of catalyst that reaches back across time and reminds us of what the arts can and should be doing in this day and age. It's what art should be about—spirit and vision instead of fame or financial gain. One of the most visionary moments for me was when you played the National Anthem unannounced, and then spun off into your improvisation—my eyes just filled with tears at your tender embrace of that fragile strand of American identity—it just bloomed into a portrait of sensitivity and compassion and perhaps even hope. Oh, for an average American to be able to be touched by such emotion! Blessings to you for bringing such beauty into this world.

Matilda

In the living room, he and I smoke the first joint. Then he leads me into the garage. My legs tingle, and each step feels like I'm walking on an inflatable floor. He's holding an almost-empty Diet Pepsi can and foraging in a cabinet. I wait, and then he manifests a small plastic bottle with dark green sludge inside. He untwists the cap. "Smell this." It smells rotten. He pours a little bit of the liquid into a Thermos cap and mixes it with some of the Diet Pepsi. "Drink." I back away. "It's safe, it's safe. Trust me. You trust me, right? Don't sip it. Just down it." I swallow the mixture like a shot as he watches. It tastes

sweet and grassy, with an alcohol warmth that curls
and grows in my stomach. I cough, eyes tearing, and
ask what's in it. "Everything." I'm immediately dazed,
watching as he licks another joint, perfecting it over an
eternity, and then, in minutes, it, too, is gone, and we're
back on the couch again. The room rotates and rocks
upward, flipping upside-down unendingly like a broken
carnival ride. I'm dizzy even though I'm sitting still, and
when I close my eyes, there's still a sense of movement.
I feel his hand grab the front of my shirt, grounding
me momentarily into some kind of equilibrium, and he
pulls me to my feet. I teeter sideways and he catches me,
dragging me into another room, still by the collar of my
shirt. He leaves me by the door and crouches beside
his bed, reaching under it, arm disappearing behind
the curtain of a hypnotizing floral comforter. I brace
myself in the doorway with both arms, swaying, my legs
buckling. He slides a long, shiny, silver case from under
his bed to his knees, unhinges it, and lifts out a rifle
to his shoulder, aiming it just next to me toward the
closet. My body begins to shake. Even my sense of what's
actually happening—*he is holding a rifle and pointing it at
me*—seems to come from far away. My vision is choppy,
images succeeding each other quickly like they're in
front of a strobe light or inside a cartoon flip book. His
face is suddenly transformed; I'm seeing a different person. The more I stare, the more unfamiliar he looks,
like how a common word can sound foreign if you say
it over and over. He's becoming an old man before my
eyes. "Now you hold it," he says, handing me the heavy
weapon. "I'll show you how." My rational mind, miles
away, watches in shock as my body submits to him and

takes the gun without protest. I'm a mannequin for him to shape and commandeer. He props the heavy rifle on my shoulder and presses my eye against the scope, and turns me so that I'm now pointing the gun into the mirror, at my reflection. His chest against my shoulder, his hips pressed against mine, I feel his legs open and I rock back, cradled there to keep my balance. The base of my spine feels warm, like it's opening to the world's beauty, letting it all in, releasing all the pain that's usually there and in every other part of my body, and all my ambition, my dreams, all those plans that make so much sense in the light of day—they all disappear. I want nothing. In fact, I'm shocked that I ever did. It all seems so absurd. So funny. He perfects the gun's position on my shoulder. "There…There. You got it. Right…*there*." I sigh, gazing at both of us through the scope, and his lips are centimeters from my ear, whispering, "It's nice, isn't it?"

Like striking the key of the piano, where, in the moment of impact, the note already begins its decay. Like driving a new car off the lot. Such was my experience of bliss at the end of America 88x50. Every wash of serenity, whether it was a beautiful vista or a feeling of community with people I met on the road or for whom I played in concert, I experienced it all sourly, as if forced to self-administer a mental pinprick to serve as a reminder that this—all the good stuff—too, would pass. I wanted to be ten steps ahead of disappointment, so I lived in that state permanently, teetering always at the edge of misery, especially in America 88x50, where my mind had to be thinking several states ahead, or in several states at once, buzzing with the sad reality that none of this would last, that this dream would indeed expire, in five, four, three, two...

And was it a waste? For the last forty-nine states, had I been so worried about generating something out of the tour, some kind of legacy that would outlive the experience and spin endlessly onward, that I'd missed the tour itself? In America 88x50 I had to function, like any artist, on the predication that I had nothing to lose. Nothing but time. But now I wondered if there was any time left at all.

Dreams can make people do dangerous things, but nothing, I suppose, is as dangerous as assuming how those dreams should come true, or worse, what will happen if they do. America 88x50 was—I had to admit it—a total dream come true; I just wasn't paying attention when it happened. And so already I could feel myself getting sucked back into its myth and legend, the seduction of America 88x50, the promise of the road, the prospect of staying out here forever because maybe *it* was still out here, that truth and power I was so desperate to find. A stocky boy in New Orleans saw it oozing out of my pores when I played, but I still imagined it waiting for me off some exit somewhere, or down one of these dusty side roads.

I thought it might be enough to come face to face with my twenty-first century America by traversing its black veins of highway for a year while earning my stripes as a pianist with a homemade fifty state tour. So why was there still all of this tangled counterpoint? Why did it still feel like I was waiting for the resolution to some long, impossible cadence?

"I'm gay." I only mouthed the words. It was as if I could only practice saying them. They still felt forbidden and hot in my chest. My stomach heaved, I gulped, and then I repeated them, saying the words almost inaudibly into the static hum of the motor. Then again, louder. "I'm gay." Then again. "I'm gay." I accelerated. "I'm gay." Faster. "I'm gay."

Onward into the endless highway[181]. I drove, until finally stopping at the gates of Death Valley. I climbed out of my Hyundai and looked out into a deep expanse of sand and blowing brush. I was alone, and leaned back to face the sun with my eyes closed, letting every sense absorb that empty desert, its empty smell, its empty sound, its empty heat, feeling its empty wind against my skin. I set my digital camera's automatic timer and placed it on the roof of the Hyundai, running back to the entrance sign and posing[182] in front of it. I was wearing my favorite t-shirt, which had nothing on it but the image of a flying pig.

PLAINFIELD, VERMONT

By now I'd had forty-nine opportunities to observe what had and hadn't worked when hosts prepared, or *didn't* prepare, for my concerts, and here in Vermont I had about a month to set things up for the final concert of the tour, in Goddard College's Haybarn Theatre, a

---

181 http://media.dissonantstates.com/i/EndlessHighway.jpg

182 http://media.dissonantstates.com/i/DeathValleyPose.jpg

benefit for Goddard's community radio station WGDR. I contacted every newspaper, radio station, and community calendar in Vermont, following up relentlessly. I created a poster[183], incorporating a collage of snapshots from the tour, and drove around Vermont affixing these posters to the glass doors of backwoods convenience stores and community bulletin boards. I promoted more than I practiced, and in less than two weeks was already hearing promos on the radio. Soon there were calendar items, newspaper articles[184], and a slew of radio interviews, including an hour-long feature on Vermont Public Radio[185].

"So where can we hear you after the tour?" the announcer asked, leaning into the microphone, and I had to think for a second. It was a tough question, here at the end of America 88x50, a tour that just sort of happened and that now was just sort of ending, with most of its evidence already packed away into boxes[186] headed for the attic.

"You'll probably hear me at your local McDonald's on the other end of the loudspeaker," I said.

The stage[187] was framed by strings of little white lights. Ceiling fans spun overhead in the cobweb-laced wooden rafters, and there were about a hundred or so chairs

183 http://media.dissonantstates.com/i/GoddardPoster.jpg

184 http://dissonantstates.com/post/13872871454/vermontarticles

185 http://media.dissonantstates.com/a/VPRCompleteBroadcast.mp3

186 http://media.dissonantstates.com/i/88x50Boxes.jpg

187 http://media.dissonantstates.com/i/GoddardStage.jpg

set up. In the front of the room, I erected two screens to play simultaneous slide shows of the tour, each starting at different points, while the pre-show music played. The Haybarn might have been filling up, but to me it seemed empty. With all the publicity, I imagined people lining the walls, but even here at home, and even with the concert proceeds benefiting a beloved community radio station, it still seemed that overall the general public still didn't dare endure a recital of modern American piano music. I felt like I knew everyone in the place. I felt my adrenaline skyrocket, and adrenaline, so I knew from experiences good and bad, could make or break a performance.

From the first notes I played, the music seemed to pour out of me with an intensity I couldn't control, like I was being dragged along in a flash flood. I was possessed, and this concert was my exorcism, the exorcism of America 88x50.

And like an exorcism, it was messy. I was playing wrong notes and blanking on passages. I was making mistakes I'd never made before in places I'd never had trouble with. I always knew, or rather, feared, that I'd mess some things up in this final concert, a concert that one might have expected, given the practice, I would play with relative ease, but I never expected it to be *this* bad. It felt like a total 360-degree return to how I had played before even my bumbling and unsure Poughkeepsie debut. This was IU. This was high school. This was amateur hour.

At intermission, I walked to the balcony behind the audience. They smiled and cheered as I passed. I wanted to cry. I wanted to start the recital over. Start the *tour* over. Start everything over. My audience dispersed into the lobby and I sat alone, not really watching anything, just staring ahead, crumbling inside. WGDR's ponytailed station manager, Bert, hopped up onto the balcony risers to meet me. "Time to start again?" I asked.

He outstretched his arms for a hug. "Fucking incredible."

I hugged him back. "Time to start again?"

"Look," he nodded toward the empty seats, "No one's back yet. Your mom set up a nice display of your newspaper clippings in the lobby. People are out there reading them."

"Well, maybe in a few minutes, then."

"Yeah, give people a little time, man." Maybe he saw my worried face, my defeated expression. "It's going great, Adam. Take it easy. Take a breath. You want to go outside? It's tough with no air conditioning in here. I don't know how you do it. I'm all wet just from hugging you!" Until then, I hadn't noticed. My clothes were sopping, and beads of sweat were rolling down my temples, down my arms, down to my hands.

It got worse.

On the last page of the Copland *Sonata*—that perfect sonic collapse at the end of the piece, that revelatory tolling, marked *elegiac*, which always brought even the most aloof listeners to attention, holding their breath until the final silence of my program, one of the first passages of the piece I'd ever learned and something I never, *ever* messed up—this was where tonight my desire to play it perfectly strangled out my concentration completely, and I found myself in a vacuum, guessing and checking, poking at the keyboard like an invalid. I'd forgotten everything. The moment was ruined. The piece was ruined. The concert. The tour. Everything. All fucking ruined.

The audience stood to their feet and clapped furiously after I made up an ending and leaned back with a defeated sigh. I had learned long ago that only by playing before an audience can a pianist really discover the truth about what they know or don't know about a piece of music, or even an entire program. So, just six days short of a year since my first America 88x50 concert, and having just played the final state and sloppiest show of the tour, I faced my truth, bowed and walked off the stage.

The hall emptied and my family and friends left for an after-party at my house. I tried gathering my things but realized that people had already taken them back to the house for me. My books. My equipment. My car keys. *My car keys?* I stood frozen. I couldn't believe it. I was stranded at the final venue of America 88x50 while a party celebrating the tour commenced without me.

I found Bert walking to his car and called my home on his flip phone. After a few tries, someone finally answered. My keys were on their way. He drove off and left me alone in the parking lot, surrounded by the darkness of the Vermont woods, the moans of the swaying trees, the songs of owls and insects, and memories of the tour—a million memories combining at once into a mass of sound and color I could barely recognize or penetrate.

Would America 88x50 become nothing more than an interesting introduction at cocktail parties, a means of convincing strangers and myself that I was actually a concert pianist? I had never believed in closure as much as I believed in getting used to things, and I feared the mediocrity I might get used to now that the tour had ended.

Trying to philosophize, I told myself that art is not about finding life's answers but about creating proof of life in the first place. I told myself that being an artist means having more confidence in one's work than in one's future. I thought of some words by Charles Ives, "consonance is relative," and told myself that it's the dissonance that defines a life, the dissonant states that an artist must suffer and savor in order to truly live. But then, all I could really hear was the wind and trees.

A custodian from inside appeared. He was tall and grizzled, wearing thick, smudged glasses. "Tonight was the biggest audience I seen in a long time," he said.

"Yeah?"

"Oh, yeah. People who play way out here don't get nearly half the audience you had. Why? You think it shoulda' been bigger?" He started to chuckle. "You said your requirement was one person."

I shrugged, my gaze down.

"Well, I'm one person," he said, "and I never heard anything like what you played tonight. That music..."

"The music—"

"I liked it," he said. "It was good. You are good. When'd you start playing?"

His words hung there for a moment until I looked up, met his eyes, and smiled, hearing tires in the distance.

"I don't know," I said. "Maybe six or seven?"

ACKNOWLEDGMENTS

This book exists only because of the people who opened their homes, venues, galleries, churches, and communities to me in America 88x50. I thank them for their trust, support, and generosity.

After six years of dancing with agents and publishers, none of whom believed this book would ever find an audience, I realized that instead of begging people to take a chance on me, I actually needed to take that chance myself. I'd like to thank Project Team 4 at CreateSpace, as well as my editors Julia and Matt, for helping guide this book to publication over the course of one year and ten proofs, the last of which I promised myself not to look at. All remaining faults are my own.

I also owe this book's development to several people in the mainstream publishing, classical music, and entertainment industry who gave it their time and input, including Charlotte Sheedy, Linda Nelson, Charles Hamlen, Francesco Sedita, and one of my closest friends on the planet, Aaron Janus.

My dear friend Justin Schier donated many selfless hours to create *The Dissonant States* blog and the online archive for this book. I bow to his virtuosic talent and unmatched patience.

Thanks to Terence O'Neil, Kevin Carter, Kenneth Wright, Alex Harper, for reading various drafts, weighing in, and keeping me positive, often against my will.

Thank you to my friends, authors Michael Fazio and Rick Whitaker, for reading the book, offering such valuable thoughts, and for going out on a limb for me when you didn't have to.

Thanks to my best friend Roy, for reading one of the earliest drafts (to his boyfriend in the car on a road trip, no less), and who has backed me up every step of the way and inspired me by example since we were ten years old.

Thanks to Beverly Scofield for continually nurturing the writer in me, and for finally giving me back that book of vignettes I wrote for her class in the seventh grade. "Miss me..."

Thanks to Rob, without whom I could never have been this honest.

Thanks to authors Wayne Hoffman, Jim Provenzano, and Blair Tindall for their publishing advice, to Vic Cardell for his cover proofreading, and to Daniela Amini and Jennifer Rubinstein for helping me refine my proposals and general idea of the book itself.

Thanks to pianists Shigeo Neriki, Frederic Chiu, Emile Naoumoff, Karen Shaw, Evelyne Brancart, Luba Dubinsky, Elaine Greenfield, Vai Meng Lei, and the inimitable, indefatigable, indestructible Richard Shadroui, for years of inspiration and guidance.

A most special thanks to Francesco Simone Savi for keeping me loved, challenged, and encouraged during the last crucial years of this book's development, and for reading several versions of it with a smile (and great feedback, actually) when I was at my least likable.

And thanks to my family for their unwavering support and love, especially my hero of a mother.

Made in the USA
San Bernardino, CA
29 November 2015